RECOGNISING FACES

RECOGNISING FACES

Vicki Bruce
Department of Psychology
University of Nottingham

LAWRENCE ERLBAUM ASSOCIATES, PUBLISHERS
Hove and London (UK)   Hillsdale (USA)

Reprinted in paperback, 1989

Lawrence Erlbaum Associates Ltd., Publishers
27 Palmeira Mansions
Church Road
Hove
East Sussex, BN3 2FA
U.K.

British Library Cataloguing in Publication Data

Bruce, Vicki
    Recognising faces.
    1. Face perception
    I. Title
    152.1'4   BF241

ISBN 0-86377-068-1 (HBK)
       0-86377-142-4 (PBK)

Typeset by Spire Print Services Ltd., Salisbury
Printed and bound by BPCC Wheatons, Exeter

To my parents,
Charles and Geraldine Bruce

Contents

Acknowledgements

This book was first drafted during the academic year of 1985–86, when I was lucky enough to be relieved of my teaching duties, thanks to a Social Science Research Fellowship from the Nuffield Foundation. I thank them most sincerely for the opportunity I was given to stand back from my research on face recognition, and to reflect upon its relationship to other areas. Some of the results of these reflections are contained within this monograph, and I am delighted that this series, "Essays in Cognitive Psychology", has provided me with the opportunity to set out the products of my deliberations.

A major aim of my year's fellowship was to spend some time in formal collaboration with my colleagues at Lancaster and Aberdeen Universities. The ideas expressed in this book have emerged from this collaboration, and have been greatly influenced by current developments at these other universities too. I thank Professors Philip Levy and Eric Salzen for their provision of space and research facilities at Lancaster and Aberdeen respectively, and I wish to say a special thank you here to my friends Andy Young and Hadyn Ellis, for their hospitality and intellectual stimulation during the year. Thanks also to Andy Ellis at Lancaster, Graham Davies at Aberdeen, and Dave Perrett at St. Andrews, for helpful discussions of some of the issues raised in this book. The Aberdeen group helped in a further way too: They allowed me the run of their research library for the duration of my visit, which enabled me to sample many of those more obscure references on facial recognition that I had always meant to read before.

Some of the experimental work which I review in Chapters 3 and 4 has been funded by the Economic and Social Research Council (grants HR 8757 and C00232247). The success of this work owes much to the care and enthusiasm of Tim Valentine who was my assistant on these projects from 1983 to 1987 and has contributed many of his own ideas to our joint work. I thank him for all his efforts. The computational work introduced in Chapter 6 is currently in its early stages, funded by a grant from the Science and Engineering Research Council (grant GR/D 8698.0). This work is in collaboration with Mike Burton, who has helped and advised me less formally, and over a much longer time period, in his dual roles as colleague and husband. I thank him for all his support and patience.

Preparation of this manuscript was considerably eased by our excellent computing facilities in the Department of Psychology at Nottingham, managed by David Dingwall. Many of the photographs which appear here were taken by Sam Grainger, our recently retired departmental photographer, and I thank him for his help in the preparation of our experimental materials over the years. David Matthews, our new photographer, produced many of the prints for this volume. The faces of many friends appear in this book. I am grateful to them for allowing me to take liberties with their appearances, but leave the reader to guess the identities of those whose faces appear here.

Parts of this manuscript have been read in draft form by Tim Brennen, Mike Burton, Glyn Humphreys, Tony Roberts, Tim Valentine, Roger Watt, and Andy Young. I thank all these people for the constructive comments that they made, and for the blunders they detected. I hope not too many remain, but of course take full responsibility for any that do.

The editorial and production staff at Lawrence Erlbaum Associates have been helpful and efficient throughout the production of this volume. Thanks to Patricia Simpson, Rohays Perry, and Michael Forster.

1 Introduction to Problems of Face Recognition

*It was only by the bumpy plane of pinkish tissue, surrounded
and tufted with hair, in which the eyes were situated, that this
creature wished to be judged, or through which it was exposed.*
Doris Lessing, *The Four Gated City*, p. 519
(MacGibbon & Kee Ltd., 1969)

RECOGNISING YOUR FRIENDS

On your way to work, out shopping or in town for the evening, you may
pass many hundreds of people—most of them complete strangers to you.
Just occasionally you will see someone you know. You might see some
local or national celebrity, seeking anonymity in the crowd. You wouldn't
normally greet such a person, but might make a mental note to tell your
family about it later. You may encounter some person whose appearance is
familiar, because you often see them at that place or time—a familiar
newspaper vendor, or someone who works in a nearby shop. You probably
wouldn't stop to say hello, but you might acknowledge the person with a
nod or other gesture of recognition, if this is mutual, and the encounter
might prompt you to buy a paper, or to remember some shopping to be got
later. By prior arrangement or quite by chance you might see a close friend,
spouse, or relative. In this situation it would appear rude not to greet them,
and you might stop for a chat, or proceed with your journey in their
company.

How do you recognise these familiar people from the crowds in which
they appear? How do you know so effortlessly not only *which* people are
familiar, but the *nature* of their familiarity, so that your social interactions
are appropriate to the degree of intimacy you share with each? We have
all, I am certain, experienced painful encounters where these recognition
processes have broken down. An apparent stranger shakes your hand
warmly and enquires about the health of your children. . . . You walk
straight past the distinguished visitor you went to meet at the station. . . .
You forget the name of your distinguished visitor when introducing her to
your boss. Such occasional embarrassments serve to emphasise the com-

plexity of the recognition and retrieval processes which normally subserve our social lives so reliably, and, as we will see later in this book, may themselves provide information about the nature of these processes.

Obviously we do not recognise people only by their faces. Voices provide important information too, though we would not normally have the information until after an encounter was initiated. In the street scenario outlined earlier, height, build, gait, and familiar clothing will all contribute to the recognition of friends and acquaintances. But many people share the same build, and similar clothes. Faces are the most reliable keys to identity, and in this book I will write almost exclusively about the recognition of "faces," rather than "people."

Although potentially reliable keys to identity, faces form a class of objects whose recognition poses a far from trivial problem of visual pattern classification. All faces must resemble each other to some extent because they have evolved to subserve such a variety of functions, which include the bearing of sense organs at appropriate places and the provision of an entry point for food, as well as the more obvious communicative functions which I discuss in the next chapter. Individual facial identity must be superimposed upon the basic pattern of the face in a way which does not impede vision, digestion, or communication, and yet makes the face unique. The result is that faces form a rather homogeneous set of patterns in which there may be very subtle differences between one individual's face and the next.

For example, the top panel of Fig. 1 shows the faces of two of my colleagues. It is really quite hard to specify the ways in which their faces differ (eye shade seems the most obvious to me), and yet we have no difficulty in deciding which of these people is shown in the lower panel of this figure, where the angle of view and accessories are changed. In this way, the figure also illustrates the next major problem in face recognition. The rather subtle distinguishing aspects of individual identity are somehow extracted across a wide variety of different poses, expressions, lighting conditions, and so forth. To date, attempts to get computers to recognise faces with anything approaching human abilities have had only limited success (see Bruce & Burton, in press, for a review). *(1989)*

Even when the critical distinctive characteristics of a face have somehow been extracted, this is still only a first stage in the identification of an individual. Somehow we then retrieve appropriate additional information about different people—where we know them from, their occupations, and their names—which enables us to interact with them appropriately. Both the processes of visual pattern classification, and those of subsequent access of information about personal identity, have apparently evolved in ways which are adaptable to the demands placed upon them by the very

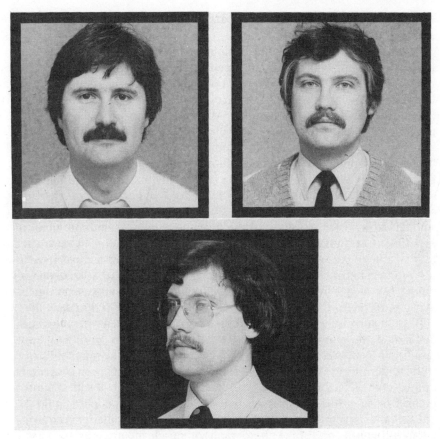

FIG. 1. It is easy to see which of these two faces from the top panel belongs to the person shown in the bottom panel, despite transformations in pose, clothing, and paraphernalia.

large societies which many humans now inhabit—societies additionally increased, in terms of identification demands, by the mass media.

In this book I describe the progress made by psychologists attempting to understand these complex processes, and point to new directions which may prove fruitful in the future. I am primarily concerned with our everyday acts of face recognition, which include the kinds of acts I outlined earlier in which we recognise familiar faces in our social environment, as well as more "passive" recognition of familiar faces in newspapers, films, or on television. I will explore how the visual information from a face is extracted, how appropriate semantic information about the personal identity of its owner is retrieved, and how access of identity from a face relates to other uses made of facial information, for example in the analysis of expression.

Before embarking on this task, I should clarify my terminology. "Recognition" is a word which has been used to cover a number of potentially different activities, and in this book I use the word recognition to include the sense of "identification." As I have already made clear, to "recognise" a face fully, more than just a sense of familiarity must be achieved. We usually recognise a face *as* someone or other, and it is this which has implications for our subsequent actions (cf. Fodor & Pylyshyn, 1981). "Recognition memory" is a much more precise term which refers to a particular experimental task. In such experiments, subjects are required to study a set of faces, and then later to "recognise" which faces, from a larger set including new faces ("distractors"), are those which were originally studied. Now, if (as is usual) all the faces used in a recognition memory experiment are unfamiliar at the beginning of the experiment, a subject may be able to perform this task on the basis of whether or not each face at test seems familiar, rather than recognising each individual as someone or other. This is one reason why a typical recognition memory experiment may give us relatively little insight into how we recognise faces in daily life.

It is not surprising, however, that the recognition memory paradigm has dominated the study of face recognition. Much of this work has been motivated by interest in the factors which contribute to the unreliability of witness identification procedures. The witnesses' task has been characterised as that of picking out the one "familiar" face from a set of photographs, or identification parade, where all the other people should be unfamiliar. The implicit assumption is that a sense of familiarity is equivalent to recognising one of the photographs or parade members as the person who perpetrated some crime. As we will see, this assumption does not necessarily hold. Since the topic of identification evidence has motivated so much of the research on face recognition, I will begin this book with a brief review of this topic.

REMEMBERING THE FACES OF STRANGERS

People other than yourself catch the same bus or train each day, or visit the same shops and restaurants regularly; your paths cross only indirectly, however, and you are unlikely to interact with, or even to notice, these people again in the future. Although you may pay cursory attention to some of those you pass by, noting a fashionable or an outrageous hairstyle, or someone's sad expression, could you recognise any of these faces if you saw them again? Suppose you were suddenly asked to describe, or to pick out from a line-up, the bus conductor you last bought a ticket from, or the checkout girl at your last visit to the supermarket. These are people you have interacted with, albeit briefly, but my guess is you would not feel confident that you could remember them, nor they you.

Police often seek descriptions from witnesses who have had the briefest of glimpses of a criminal, and they may ask a witness to help construct a likeness of the wanted person, or to try to select him (it is usually a him) from a book of mug-shots. Once they have apprehended a subject, the witness may be asked to try to identify him from a line-up. The police are motivated by their need to collect the best available evidence in an attempt to solve a crime. It is perhaps not surprising that they place so much weight on facial description and identification evidence to this end. What should surprise us more is the willingness and confidence with which witnesses will describe or attempt to identify faces that have been viewed in less than ideal circumstances.

The fallibility of eye-witness testimony is now a major area of applied cognitive psychology (e.g. see reviews by Clifford & Bull, 1978; Loftus, 1979; Yarmey, 1979) and no attempt will be made here to review the area. I will, however, illustrate some of the problems inherent in witness identification procedures by mentioning a couple of cases which contributed to public concern about this matter during the 1970s. Shepherd, Ellis, and Davies (1982) and Devlin (1976) provide further details of these British examples.

PROBLEMS WITH IDENTIFICATION PARADES

In 1973 George Ince was tried for murder in a case which rested almost entirely on identification evidence. The two key witnesses had survived an armed robbery in which both had been injured, but both had viewed the murderer for at least 20 minutes, which might lead us to expect them to be able to identify their assailant with some accuracy.

George Ince, a man with previous convictions for robbery, and under suspicion for further offences, was apprehended and placed in an identity parade. The witnesses were the owner of the raided restaurant, whose wife had been killed in the attack, and his daughter. The father failed to pick Ince out of the parade, but the daughter did identify him. However, it later transpired that the daughter had been shown photographs of Ince on several occasions prior to the parade. Furthermore, she had failed to make more than a "partial" identification of Ince from photographs when first shown them.

This case highlights several problems of witness identification. Although both the witnesses had had a long view of the criminal, both were under considerable stress both during and after the incident in which the mother was killed and they were hurt. The effects of a life-threatening situation on memory are not known, but the effects on their motivation to see the murderer apprehended are surely both predictable and understandable. In the event, however, the father did not identify the suspect, and the daughter identified the man with whose photograph she was already highly familiar.

Ince was discharged at a second trial where his girlfriend provided him with an alibi. However, he was to have further problems with identification parades. He was eventually brought to trial for a bullion robbery for which he was under suspicion at the time of the murder trial. Several civilian witnesses had failed to identify him, but two policemen did pick him out from a line-up—six months after they had glimpsed the robbers while pursuing them. It transpired that both officers had seen photographs of Ince prior to the parade. In both of Ince's trials, procedures were in direct breach of 1969 regulations stating that witnesses should not be shown photographs of a suspect prior to an identification parade.

Ince's face was undoubtedly familiar to the witnesses who identified him in connection with the murder and the bullion robbery, and as the only "familiar face" in the line-up, would inevitably be more likely to be selected. It is unlikely, however, that the witnesses would have been able to tell whether his face was familiar because of a connection with the original incident, or whether it was familiar only from the photographs which had been shown prior to the parade. The circumstances in which a face was encountered are much less well remembered than the fact that it has been encountered before (Brown, Deffenbacher, & Sturgill, 1977). A satisfactory witness identification requires that the witness recognises the face as that of the person seen perpetrating the crime, and any encounter with the suspect, whether in photographs or in the flesh, which intervenes between the original incident and the parade can only serve to invalidate the parade.

The second case I will mention is one in which a number of witnesses—both civilian and police—confidently, but mistakenly, picked the same man as the person responsible for an attempted theft from parking meters and subsequent armed offences during the ensuing pursuit. Laszlo Virag was convicted on the basis of identification evidence alone, and, it later transpired, he was convicted wrongly. There were 17 witnesses, 6 of them police, and, of these, 8 (including 5 police) picked Mr. Virag from parades which appear to have been composed and conducted fairly, although even in this case the 3 civilian witnesses who identified Virag had earlier identified him from photographs. What is surprising about this case is the confidence and consistency with which Virag was mistakenly identified. One police witness was reported as saying (Devlin, 1976, p. 47): "his face is imprinted on my brain." This case highlights a different problem—that of unreliability of witnesses who may appear confident and consistent with one another. In this case, a man called Georges Payen was brought under suspicion for the offences for which Laszlo Virag was convicted, and an early observation by one of the police officers on the case noted that the two men were (Devlin, 1976, p. 55): "in no way similar in appearance and it is therefore difficult to believe that all these witnesses could have been mistaken." The interested reader is referred to the Devlin report where photographs of both men are shown (Devlin, 1976, p. 66), and I will return to consider the nature of their resemblance (to me more striking than their differences), later in the book.

In neither of these cases is there any suspicion that the police were deliberately biasing witnesses prior to an identification parade. Blatant unfairness (see Buckhout, 1974, for some examples) gives cause for other kinds of concern. My point here is to emphasise the fragility of a memory for a previously unfamiliar face, seen in perceptually and emotionally unsatisfactory circumstances, yet upon which a conviction for a serious crime may be based. We need to understand the way in which such fragile memories may form the basis of sincerely offered, but mistaken evidence.

The Devlin report understandably prompted much research aimed directly at revealing the limits of eyewitness performance. What are the effects of exposure duration, delay between incident and parade, and the emotional impact of the witnessed scene on the likely accuracy of a witness's memory? What effects do the mode of identification, composition of the parade, and nature of instructions given to witnesses have on their likelihood of making an incorrect selection? A considerable amount of valuable research has addressed these questions, much of it summarised in Shepherd et al. (1982).

As well as applied research aimed directly at understanding the task faced by a witness to a crime, the Devlin report served also to stimulate more widespread research into recognition memory for faces. Such cases of mistaken identity highlighted an apparent paradox, since memory for faces under laboratory conditions was generally found to be very accurate (e.g. Brown et al., 1977, found that subjects were able to recognise 96% of faces studied two days earlier) and usually more accurate than the recognition of other kinds of familiar objects (see Ellis, 1975, for a review). Why is there such a discrepancy between apparently high face recognition memory in the laboratory, and poor performance in the field? What factors reduce performance in the laboratory? Are these the same as factors which affect memory generally, or is there something "special" about face recognition? Between them, the laboratory and the applied studies have furnished us with a wealth of "facts" about recognition memory for unfamiliar faces. Not all these "facts" are relevant to eyewitness testimony, but all must be accommodated by any emergent theory of face recognition.

R.F.—B

FACTS ABOUT FACE RECOGNITION MEMORY

In a typical face recognition memory experiment, subjects study faces and then must select, from a larger set of faces, the face or faces which they originally studied. Unless a "forced choice" procedure is used, which results in a single percent correct score, recognition memory performance is usually assessed both in terms of the number of originally studied "targets" that are correctly recognised (hit rate) and the number of novel "distractor" faces that are incorrectly recognised (false positive rate). Hits and false positives are often combined in some way to give a composite score of recognition, but are sometimes reported and analysed separately. In much of this book I will talk generally about factors which "improve" or "reduce" the accuracy of recognition memory, without being specific about the measures used in the respective studies. Where I am vague, I will be referring to effects on overall (composite score) accuracy, and will refer specifically to effects on hits or false positives only where these have important consequences.

Many of the factors which influence face recognition are common to memory in general. Thus, as examples, increasing the exposure duration of each target (Bruce and Valentine, in press; Ellis, Davies, & Shepherd, 1977; Laughery, Alexander, & Lane, 1971; Light, Kayra-Stuart, & Hollander, 1979) and decreasing target-distractor similarity (Davies, Shepherd, & Ellis, 1979; Laughery, Fessler, Leronovitz, & Yoblick, 1974; Patterson & Baddeley, 1977) both serve to increase the accuracy with which targets can be selected correctly. Further examples of apparent similarities between effects found with faces and those which operate generally in memory come from the study of context effects in face recognition, and the beneficial effects of encouraging semantic processing of the faces at study (see Memon & Bruce, 1985 for a review). We will consider these effects in detail in Chapter 4.

Of more immediate interest here are effects of variables which either have no parallels in the literature on memory for words or other comparison materials, or which appear to show different effects when faces are tested.

Delay

A number of experiments have reported no effects of delays of weeks or even months between study and test on a person's ability to recognise previously presented faces. Using a single target face, Laughery et al. (1971) found that varying the study-test delay from 4 minutes to 1 week had little effect on performance, and Laughery and Fowler (1976) found the recognition of a single target to remain at 100% after 6 months delay.

Egan, Pittner, and Goldstein (1977) found no decrease in hit rate, but increased false positive rate, as delay was varied from 2 days to 56 days. Using multiple targets, Chance, Goldstein, and McBride (1975) found no difference between performance at immediate test and that after a 48-hour delay; Laughery et al. (1974) found no difference between immediate testing and a week's delay.

However, detrimental effects of delay have been observed in some studies. Shepherd and Ellis (1973) found that performance on faces of "moderate" attractiveness (but not on faces of high or low attractiveness) declined over a 35-day delay, and Davies, Ellis, and Shepherd (1978a) found subjects were poorer at recognising the face of a single target if they were tested three weeks later, compared with two days after presentation. Memon (Note 5) found recognition memory performance was poorer after a delay both in an experiment using multiple photographic targets (comparing immediate testing with a delay of 1 week), and in an experiment involving a single filmed target (comparing performance at 45 minutes with that at 1 week after presentation) in a task more like that of an eyewitness.

What seems clear from the above studies is that face recognition is by no means inevitably made worse by a delay. What seems more important than the passage of time per se is the nature of encounters with other faces during that interval. Laughery et al. (1971) found that the position of the target face in the test list had far more dramatic effects than those of delay. If the target was early on in the series, it was well recognised. If it was late, it was rarely spotted. Thus, interference from faces in the same context as the target face appears much more powerful than interference from faces outside the laboratory episode. An encounter with a face seems to be tightly bound to the context in which it was seen, and this is a topic to which we will return in Chapter 4.

Exposure Mode

Laboratory studies of facial recognition typically present subjects with photographs of faces to remember. Shepherd et al. (1982) report an experiment in which one of two targets was presented live, on colour video or on still colour or monochrome photographs, and recognition was tested using live, video, or still identification parades. They found no effect of parade mode, but presentation mode did show an effect, with live presentation leading to superior performance compared with video or still presentation, which did not differ. The superiority of viewing a live target cannot be attributed to motion or to colour, since the video condition included both these elements. The fact that there was no apparent advantage of video over monochrome photographic presentation (a result we have replicated in Nottingham [Bruce & Valentine, in press]) suggests that such information does not contribute much to our memory for a face. What seems possible, particularly in the incidental learning situation employed by Shepherd et al. (where subjects at "study" were required to assess whether the target was telling the truth), is that a live person may engage the subject in a kind of social interaction not elicited by filmed or photographed presentation. When a person talks to us we behave differently from the way we behave when we watch a film. This is an important factor which is missing from almost all reported work on face perception conducted by cognitive, as opposed to social, psychologists.

Transformation Between Presentation and Test

While many early studies of face recognition reported astonishingly high rates of facial recognition performance (see Ellis, 1975 for a review), in most of these tasks subjects were tested with the same photographs of the targets as those used in the study phase. Such experiments may confound true facial recognition (which should generalise to different views and expressions) with picture recognition (Bruce, 1982; Hay & Young, 1982). We know that people are phenomenally good at recognising large sets of novel pictures (Shepard, 1967; Standing, Conezio, & Haber, 1970). While there is some evidence to suggest that recognition of faces is better than that of other homogeneous categories of familiar items, such as houses or canine faces (Scapinello & Yarmey, 1970; Yin, 1969), it is impossible to compare adequately levels of performance without controls over relative degrees of target-distractor similarity (Ellis, 1975). Houses could undoubtedly be better recognised than faces if targets and distractors were suitably manipulated.

It is therefore more legitimate, and of more theoretical interest, to investigate how well faces can be remembered following various transformations in their appearance between study and test, and, where appropriate, to compare the effects of such transformations on face recognition with their effects on the recognition of other materials. The transformation which has received the most attention in this respect is that of *inversion*.

Upside-down faces are disproportionately difficult to recognise. Yin's (1969) study is most often cited. He found that recognition memory for upright faces was better than that for pictures of houses, aeroplanes, or schematic men-in-motion, but when all materials were inverted, performance on faces became worse than that on other materials. Similar results were found by Scapinello and Yarmey (1970), who compared recognition memory for human faces with that for canine faces and buildings.

The disproportionate effect of inversion on face recognition has been taken as an important piece of evidence to suggest that faces are processed by special mechanisms, not shared by other materials (Ellis, 1975; Hay & Young, 1982, provide critical reviews of this position). One criticism of the studies by Yin and Scapinello and Yarmey, however, is that the comparison materials are in no way as familiar and important everyday objects as are faces (e.g. see Goldstein & Chance, 1981). Perhaps the disproportionate effect of inversion is a consequence of our disproportionate exposure to upright faces—the more familiar are items in one orientation, the more they will suffer if this is changed, since the perceptual skills developed for upright faces may transfer negatively to inverted faces. A further criticism is that the cited studies looked at facial recognition confounded with picture recognition—faces were presented and tested in identical poses.

Tim Valentine and I (Valentine & Bruce, 1986a; also Valentine, Note 7) recently attempted to clarify the basis of the inversion effect. In one experiment, we compared the effects of inverting white and black faces on recognition memory performance by white subjects. White subjects are generally less good at recognising black faces (see later section), arguably because they are less familiar with them. And in our experiment, exposure duration in the upright face condition had to be increased for black faces in order to equate performance on upright black and white faces. If the effect of inversion on upright white faces is due to their special familiarity in that orientation, then inverting black faces should show less of an effect. In fact, we found the opposite: Recognition of black faces was more impaired by inversion than recognition of white faces. The effect of inversion cannot simply be attributed to "familiarity" without further qualification.

In the same series of experiments (Valentine & Bruce, 1986a) we also replicated Yin's initial result, but in a situation where the pictures of the faces, and the houses which served as comparison materials, were changed between presentation and test, thus increasing the generality of the observed effect. Finally, we tested Yin's own explanation of the inversion effect—that upside-down faces are hard to recognise because their expressions cannot be interpreted. No evidence was found to support this. Subjects encouraged to judge the personalities of the faces at study, and hence presumably attending to their expressions, were no more affected by inversion of the faces at test than were subjects who were encouraged to attend to particular physical features of the faces.

The inversion effect thus appears robust, but difficult to explain in terms of familiarity or the encoding of expression (see also Valentine, Note 7). However, it appears not to be a "face-specific" effect, but one which is perhaps an inevitable consequence of a particular level of perceptual "expertise" developed for a particular kind of visual shape. Diamond and Carey (1986) have shown that dog breeders given a task of recognition memory for particular, individual dogs, are more adversely affected than nonexperts if the dog pictures are inverted. Later in this book (Chapter 3) I will return to consider how we might accommodate this observation alongside the effects of inversion on other-race faces reported by Valentine and Bruce (1986a).

The observed effects of inversion (and related effects of reversal to or from photographic negative [e.g. Galper & Hochberg, 1971; Phillips, 1972]) may be of some theoretical interest to researchers of face processing, but they are not transformations which are typically important in tasks of remembering faces outside the laboratory. Of more relevance here are effects of changes in *pose* and/or *expression* between study and test phases. Until recently, it was often reported that recognition memory for faces was unaffected by moderate transformations in view (say from full face to ¾) between study and test. This claim was based on the results of two studies by Davies, Ellis, and Shepherd (1978b) and Patterson and Baddeley (1977). Since then, however, there have been numerous reports of effects of even very small changes in picture. My own study (Bruce, 1982) serves as an example. I obtained pictures of academic staff in my own and other departments at Nottingham University, each shown in full face and ¾ view, in smiling and neutral expressions. In one experiment, one view of each of 24 of these people was shown for study by subjects unfamiliar with the faces. Subjects were informed that in a later memory test, the pictures shown of the people might be changed, so that they should try to remember the person and not the picture. At test, the 24 targets were intermixed with 24 distractor items. Eight of the targets reappeared in the same view, 8 were changed in either pose or expression, and 8 were changed in both pose and expression. The observed hit rate was 90% for unchanged faces, 76% for faces with a change in pose or expression, and 60.5% for faces where both pose and expression were changed. Recognition latencies followed the same trend, with changed faces leading to slower recognition than unchanged faces. In a second experiment, the faces were studied by psychology student subjects who knew half the people whose faces appeared (the psychology lecturers). While recognition accuracy was very much higher for the familiar than for the unfamiliar faces, an effect of changing the view between presentation and test was observed on the recognition latencies for the familiar faces, showing even more convincingly that details of particular pictures are retained in memory and can influence subsequent recognition memory performance. In Chapter 5, I will consider how an "instance-based" model of memory (e.g. McClelland & Rumelhart, 1985) might accommodate such effects more naturally than the "abstractive" framework presented by Bruce and Young (1986), and discussed at length in Chapter 4.

A transformation which is directly relevant to the task sometimes faced by an eyewitness is that created by disguising the face through change of hairstyle, addition of spectacles, and so forth (see Fig. 2). Patterson and

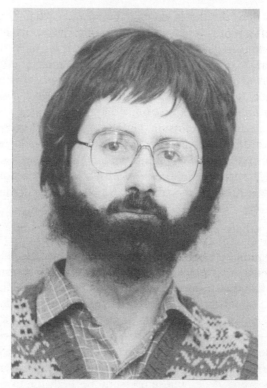

FIG. 2. One of the men from Fig. 1 in disguise.

Baddeley (1977) found that recognition memory was severely affected by disguise of faces between presentation and test, with different components of disguise appearing to act in a cumulative manner. Adding a wig and a beard reduced recognition performance more than adding a wig or beard alone. Davies and Flin (1984) looked at the effectiveness of the stocking mask often employed by criminals as an easy disguise at the time of the incident. They were able to show that this appears to operate through the distortion (squashing) of facial features, rather than through the reduction of facial detail by the mesh of the stocking. They showed this by demonstrating that targets disguised with polythene bags (!) were as poorly remembered as those wearing textured stockings, while targets viewed through a nondistorting mesh were as well remembered as undisguised targets.

A further transformation which may occur between presentation and test is a change in the mode of presentation of the faces. A witness may view a live face, but then be required to attempt to recognise the person from photographs. Alternatively, a "wanted" poster may appear in a police station, where the criminal is then to be spotted from "live" everyday encounters. Using a variety of presentation and test modes, most researchers have shown that recognition performance is better if study and test modes are the same than if they differ. Thus Patterson (1978), using filmed and still presentation and test, found that performance was better if faces were studied and tested in film, or in photographs, than if study and test mode were different. Davies et al. (1987b) found similar effects where presentation and test mode were varied from line drawings to photographs. An interaction between study and test mode is not always found, however. Shepherd et al. (1982) found a main effect of presentation mode, with live targets better remembered than filmed or photographed ones, but no apparent interaction with the mode in which the parade was conducted.

Stimulus and Subject Variables

In the foregoing discussion, we have ignored differences in the memorability of individual faces, or in the mnemonic powers of different subjects. Faces are not all equally easy to remember, and a factor which has recently attracted some attention is that of the *distinctiveness* of faces on their memorability. A "distinctive" face is one whose visual appearance is relatively unusual compared with the set of faces under consideration. (This comparison set must be defined for a particular task—a single female face would be a distinctive item in a recognition memory experiment where all other faces were male, but might not be a distinctive female face compared with female faces generally.) Light et al. (1979) found that faces rated as "typical" yielded lower hit rates and higher false positive rates than those rated as "unusual." This appeared to be an effect of the physical distinctiveness of the face, since these "typical" faces were seen as more similar to other faces in the pool used than were the "unusual" faces.

Differential distinctiveness of faces is the most parsimonious way of encompassing several other effects in the literature which might otherwise be given a very different kind of explanation. For example, Mueller, Heesacker, and Ross (1984) attributed the differential memorability of faces rated as "likeable" and "unlikeable" to their differential visual distinctiveness rather than to affective factors, and Mueller and Thompson (Note 6) found that differences in the memorability of faces rated in terms of apparent "honesty" could also be attributed to variations in distinctiveness. As we will see in Chapter 3, distinctiveness can also be shown to affect the speed of recognising highly familiar faces, and may thus be revealing about the way in which faces are encoded for recognition.

Many other factors which differentiate faces can be shown to have effects which interact with subject factors. For example, while it has sometimes been reported that women are better than men at recognising faces, more often this is observed in an interaction with the sex of face—women are especially good at recognising female faces (see Shepherd, 1981, for a review). However, sex effects are often not observed at all, and where they are statistically significant, they are nonetheless small in size.

A much more powerful combination of stimulus and subject factors comes when we consider effects of *race* of faces and subjects. In almost all published studies (again, see Shepherd's 1981 review) it has been found that people are poorer at recognising faces from a different race than they are at recognising faces of their own race. This does not seem to be attributable to differences in the variability of faces in different races (i.e. it does not appear to be the case that Chinese or Japanese faces are more like one another than are Caucasian faces; Goldstein & Chance, 1978; 1979), but seems more likely to be due to lack of familiarity with the salient distinguishing characteristics of different race faces. However, attempts to train observers to become more proficient at remembering the faces of other races have been rather disappointing (Malpass, 1981, reviews this area).

These then are some of the factors which may influence face recognition memory, and some of them may play important roles in eyewitness memory. While my main aim in this book is to examine the processes involved in everyday recognition of familiar faces, the hope is that we may be able to develop a theoretical framework which can encompass the task of remembering laboratory episodes as well as that of identifying our friends. The key demand of any face recognition task, whether in the laboratory or in the street, is to get from the available visual information to an adequate semantic specification. In Chapter 4 we will consider possible theories of this process. First, however, through consideration of the applied problem of face *recall*, we introduce a perhaps more fundamental problem—that of how the visual pattern which we call a "face" should be described.

TECHNIQUES FOR FACE RECONSTRUCTION

All the earlier discussion has focused on factors which may influence how well we can recognise a face. What of face recall? It is obviously difficult to recall a face in words, and we certainly cannot ask most people to produce a drawing of a remembered face. One way to construct a face is to furnish an artist with a set of verbal descriptions, and then suggest modifications to the produced drawing. A second technique, which has been used increasingly by police forces in the U.S.A., the United Kingdom, and elsewhere, is to help the witness to construct a remembered face using a kit of pre-drawn

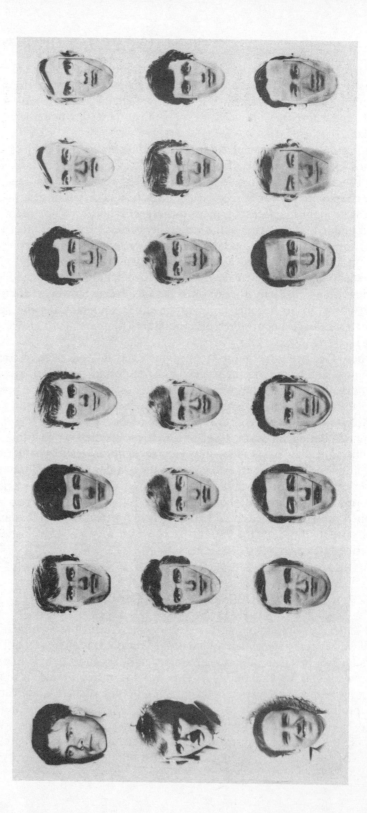

FIG. 3. Examples of attempted Photofit reconstruction. Each row shows a target face (at the left) and reconstructions of it made by different observers, from memory, immediately after viewing the target. In each row, the left-hand group of Photofit constructions were judged as better likenesses of the targets than the right-hand group. Reproduced from Ellis, Shepherd, and Davies (1975) with permission from the authors and the British Psychological Society.

17

or photographed features. The Identikit system which is used in the U.S.A. originally comprised a set of line-drawn features, but has recently been replaced with a photographed version, much like the Photofit. In this chapter, and elsewhere in this book, I will use the term Identikit only to refer to the line-drawn version.

The assumption behind the marketing and use of a kit is that it is more economical and convenient than using the main alternative—a police sketch artist—while resulting in more acceptable likenesses than witnesses could produce themselves through drawing. However, until relatively recently, little in the way of formal evaluation of the kits' effectiveness had been conducted. During the 1970s, a team in the U.S.A. led by Laughery evaluated the effectiveness of Identikit at about the same time as the Aberdeen group in Scotland was examining Photofit. The results obtained by the two groups with their respective kits were remarkably similar.

In the Laughery study (Laughery, Duval, & Fowler, 1977; Laughery & Fowler, 1980), pairs of "witnesses" viewed a target person for several minutes before one witness attempted to construct the face using Identikit and the other worked with a sketch artist. To provide a baseline assessment of the optimum performance of their respective reconstructive mediums, the Identikit technician and the sketch artist each produced constructions of each of the different targets used in the study with the target in view. All constructions were then rated according to their likeness to the target. Laughery et al. found that sketches resulted in better overall likenesses than did Identikit constructions, and that only the sketches showed a difference in rated likeness between constructions made from witness descriptions and those done with the target in view. This result does not reflect a strength of the Identikit, but a weakness—performance with the Identikit was not good enough to be sensitive to the effect of removing the target from view.

The Aberdeen group obtained similar results. Davies et al. (1978a) found that rated accuracy of Photofit likenesses (Fig. 3 shows some examples) was not influenced by a week's delay between observation and construction. Ellis, Davies, and Shepherd (1978) found no difference in the accuracy of Photofits made with the target in view and those made from memory. Perhaps most worrying of all was Ellis et al.'s (1978) observation that witnesses' own drawings of targets in view were rated as considerably better likenesses than were their Photofit constructions—i.e. an accurate *copy* of a face is extremely difficult to produce with these kits. From memory, the Photofit was marginally superior to sketches, since the witnesses' drawing abilities deteriorated dramatically when drawing from memory rather than copying. Nonetheless the results, drawn in Fig. 4, do not present the kits in good light.

Why should Identikit and Photofit yield such poor objective perfor-

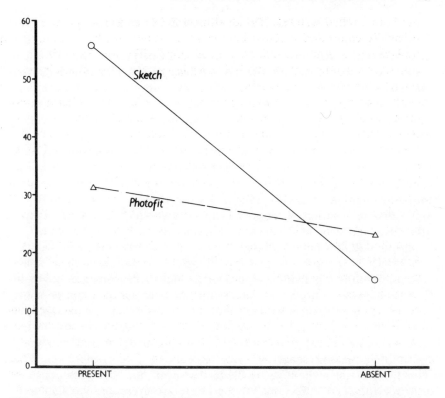

FIG. 4. Mean rated likeness (out of 100 maximum) of witnesses' own sketches and Photofit constructions made either in the presence of the target or from memory. Drawn from data in Ellis et al., 1978.

mance on facial recall? One contributing factor is the limited number of features and face shapes, etc. available in the kits, but another is undoubtedly in the nature of the construction task itself. Use of a kit *assumes* that a witness can decompose a face into its constituent eyes, nose, and mouth—an assumption which Penry (1971), Photofit's inventor, sees as the explicit basis of face perception itself.

The problems which have been revealed in the evaluation of Photofit have demonstrated to us that however it is that we store faces for recognition purposes, it is not in a manner which is compatible with the task of decomposing them into their constituent features. The need to develop more adequate aids to facial reconstruction is one motivation for developing an account of how the visual features of faces are represented within our memories, and by what processes we access these representations. This is a topic which will be addressed in Chapter 3, and again in Chapter 6 of this book.

THE RATIONALE AND PLAN OF THIS BOOK

Most of the research into face recognition conducted during the 1970s had a distinctly atheoretical air, largely because of the climate which was created by issues of eyewitness fallibility. In contrast, my own work, and that of some of my colleagues, has been motivated by the need to develop some kind of theoretical framework to guide research into face recognition.

This book charts the progress of this theoretical development. In Chapter 2, I place the task of recognising the identity of faces in its social context, and discuss how the recognition of the identity of a face is related to the recognition of its expression, its attractiveness, and so forth. I will argue that recognition of identity is an activity which is independent of other uses made of facial information, and, as such, may be explained independently. In Chapter 3 I then review what we have learned about the way in which we process facial patterns to extract from them some description of their individuating properties, before describing at length, in Chapter 4, how we proceed to access further information about personal identity. Chapter 4 is really the meat of this sandwich, since it presents the theoretical state of the art at the time this book was conceived—in the form of a theoretical framework which has already proved extremely valuable in making sense of some aspects of face recognition. The framework is not without its problems, however, and it is in response to these that potential directions for the future are presented in Chapters 5 and 6.

The theoretical ideas developed in the book have emerged in collaboration with a number of other people, notably colleagues in Nottingham, Lancaster, and Aberdeen, and have grown out of the results of empirical studies of a number of different kinds. I have invested much of my own effort into studying the recognition of highly familiar faces, in order to understand better our everyday acts of face recognition, using methods which resemble those used to study word recognition and semantic memory. In this volume, I will draw most heavily upon the kind of evidence to which I have contributed, i.e. evidence derived from experiments with normal adult subjects. Neuropsychological evidence has also been important in guiding our thinking, but I will draw upon it only to emphasise the convergence of evidence from different approaches, or where experimental evidence is lacking or inconclusive.

Although I will not review neuropsychological findings in any detail, it is probably in the neuropsychological field that the framework developed in Chapter 4 finds its most obvious potential application—by allowing us to consider the nature of a particular deficit and hence to suggest a remedial programme. However, in developing this theory, I am not losing sight of the forensic issues raised in this chapter. It is my belief that when we have a better idea of the way in which we represent faces in memory, we may be able to design better reconstructive aids than the kits currently available, and also to understand the nature of the visual resemblance which could lead Mr. Virag to be mistaken for Mr. Payen (see p. 7). At the end of this book, I will return to consider whether what we have learned will shed light upon such problems.

2 Affective and Communicative Aspects of Face Perception

Faces are much more than just useful keys to individual identity. Many other kinds of meaning may be derived from the visual pattern of the face. Faces serve as signals for underlying emotional states through their portrayal of facial expression; the perception of lip and tongue movements helps to disambiguate speech, and a variety of other facial gestures may serve both affective and communicative functions during personal interaction. The effective use of eye contact is an important component of social skills (Argyle, 1983; Argyle & Cooke, 1976), and pupil size is an index of arousal (see Goldwater, 1972, for a review).

So important is the face in our interpersonal communication, that face perception is as much the domain of the social as the cognitive psychologist. Indeed, at a recent meeting of British psychologists researching face perception, the eminent social psychologist Michael Argyle expressed surprise that cognitive psychologists were working on face processing at all. To him, it was an area of social psychology. Expression perception, perceived attractiveness and liking, stereotypical attribution, and cross-cultural comparisons of facial gestures are among the many topics in social psychology which involve research on aspects of face processing. The social psychology of face perception tackles applied problems too. Argyle (1983) describes how training in the display and perception of nonverbal communicative signals may improve social skills, and we may learn more about the possible reasons for certain outcomes of telephone negotiations through understanding the role which nonverbal communication normally plays in social interaction (Morley & Stephenson, 1977).

In this chapter I will review very briefly selected aspects of the social perception of faces, in order to emphasise the variety and complexity of the different inferences which may be drawn from varying facial patterns. It may be because the communicative power of the face makes it a focus of attention during social interaction that the face has become the part of the body which also reveals an individual's identity. Nevertheless, despite this possible evolutionary interdependence of the different signalling functions of the face, there is good evidence, which I present at the end of this chapter, that the recognition of facial identity is a process which proceeds independently from the recognition of facial expression and facial speech. This clarification of the relationship between facial recognition and other social cognitions based upon the face serves as an important theoretical starting point, and is an essential prerequisite to the further elaboration of face recognition processes presented in the later chapters of this book.

EXPRESSION PERCEPTION

I am forever passing people on the street who say "Cheer up, it might never happen." Clearly, though quite unintentionally, I tend to wear a troubled face. Now we can ask two questions about the perception of expression. The first is how do we perceive and categorise facial expressions, and the second is how accurately can we deduce the emotions which underly such expressions. With respect to my own anecdote, we can enquire both about the perception of a sad or worried expression and also about whether this is giving *accurate* information about the emotional state of the person wearing it. It is the first question which holds most interest here. The classification of facial expressions is a necessary prerequisite for the inference of emotion, but the latter will involve other factors as well.

The research techniques used to examine expression perception have changed little since Darwin's (1872) painstaking research (Salzen, 1981), with the vast majority of studies until quite recently examining the perception of posed expressions in static photographs like those shown in Fig. 5 (e.g. Frijda, 1969; Osgood, 1966; Plutchik, 1962; Tomkins & McCarter, 1964; Woodworth, 1938). Ekman, Friesen, and Ellsworth (1982a) review these studies and find a high degree of consistency in the emotion categories which can be assigned to such posed expressions. They propose that the combined evidence points to seven categories which can be discriminated: happiness, surprise, fear, sadness, anger, disgust/contempt, and interest. They also present evidence that these are *universal* categories, understood by members of all literate and preliterate cultures. The results of several studies point to this conclusion. One of the clearest demonstrations was that by Ekman and Friesen (1971) of natives of New Guinea. Their subjects were told a story and asked to pick the face, from a set of three photographs, which went with the story (i.e. the one which appeared to display an appropriate emotion). Adults and children showed a high degree of agreement with the pictures which would have been selected by members of our own culture in such a task.

The use of posed expressions has many potential drawbacks, and, more recently, researchers have made increasing use of spontaneous expressions. However, all such research has been directed toward the question of how accurately spontaneous expressions inform us about underlying emotional states. Reviewing such studies, Ekman, Friesen, and Ellsworth (1982b)

 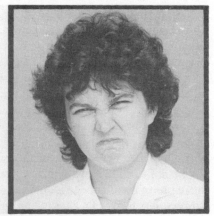

FIG. 5. Most research on the perception of facial expressions has made use of posed expressions like these attempts at surprise, disgust, and happiness.

suggest that observers can accurately distinguish at least positive from negative emotional states from facial information. Taken together, the results from posed and spontaneous expressions suggest that in our everyday acts of face perception we may be able to distinguish several different kinds of expression, and that these distinctions are sufficient at least for us to tell whether the people we view are feeling positive or negative.

What information allows us to categorise expressions? Ekman and Friesen (1978; 1982) have produced a comprehensive system for describing all possible visually distinguishable movements of the face. The system, called the "Facial Action Coding System," or FACS, is based on the enumeration of all the "action units" of the face which give rise to visible facial movements. An action unit is very roughly equivalent to a particular muscle in the face, whose activation gives rise to a noticeable facial change. The correspondence between action units and muscle units is approximate because some muscles give rise to more than one action unit (Ekman and Friesen give as an example the frontalis muscle, which raises the brow—this is separated into two action units depending on whether its inner or outer part raises the inner or outer part of the eyebrow), and some action units may be produced by the actions of different muscles, which are not visibly distinct from each other. Examples of the action units involved in eyebrow motions are shown in Fig. 6 (though note that the presentation of such "frozen" actions is a less than satisfactory use of a system developed to code movements rather than frozen postures). It is possible to make use of this figure to identify the action units in the brows shown in the expressions in Fig. 5.

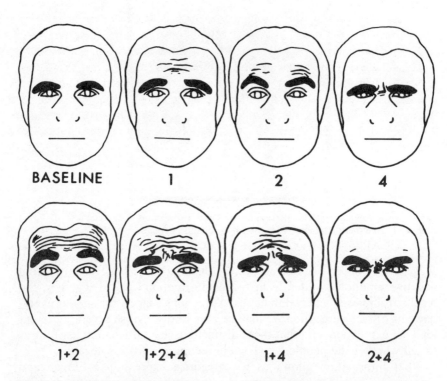

FIG. 6. The different action units for the brow and forehead identified by the Facial Action Coding System (Ekman & Friesen, 1978). Action units 1, 2, and 4 may occur alone (top) or in combination (bottom). Different action units and combinations are associated with different expressions. For example, action unit 1 alone indicates sadness, but 1 with 2 indicates surprise (cf. Figure 5). These drawings were obtained by tracing photographs, and are reproduced from Ekman (1979) with permission of the author and publishers.

Using FACS, any complex set of facial movements (including, presumably, those involved in facial speech) may be described as involving particular components, and Ekman and Friesen (1982) present data which suggest that different observers can make reasonably reliable use of such a coding system. The validity of the system as an index of facial emotion has been demonstrated in a number of studies. Ekman, Friesen, and Ancoli (1980) for example, showed that hypotheses about experienced emotions derived from FACS corresponded to the emotions subjects actually reported experiencing after viewing pleasant and unpleasant films.

Facial animation artists have made use of FACS in the development of computer-animated figures. Platt and Badler (1981) made use of FACS notation to manipulate a model of facial muscle structure which drove changes in expression of a face model, and recently Waters (Note 9) has extended this approach in a way which is not specific to the topology of a particular face.

Unfortunately, despite all the effort in the development of FACS as a tool for describing facial movement, there has been rather little exploration of the question of whether "action units" are the units whereby we categorise expressions. Ekman and Friesen (1978, cited in Ekman et al., 1982a) claim that emotions which are often confused with one another are those which share many action units. However, there appears to have been rather little systematic investigation of this, nor any comparison of whether a different basis for description (of the postures or relative positions of facial features, for example [see Pilowsky, Thornton, & Stokes, 1986]) would be better or worse at accounting for such confusions.

FACIAL SPEECH

When a person speaks, there is movement of the lips, tongue, jaws, and cheeks. Although we can obviously understand speech via the telephone or radio, where none of these movements is visible, there is some quite persuasive evidence suggesting that lipreading may play a role in the perception of speech. Obviously deaf people may learn to rely entirely on lipreading to comprehend speech, but Campbell (in press) has argued that those with normal hearing may also make use of information in lip and tongue movements. Her argument is based in part upon the way in which we are disturbed when lip movements are out of synchrony with speech (as in a poorly dubbed film) and by our susceptibility to the McGurk illusion (McGurk & MacDonald, 1976). In this illusion, an observer is shown a mouthed phoneme shape which differs from that which should correspond to a heard phoneme, and may perceive a phoneme which is a blend of the two. More direct evidence for the use of lipreading in normal speech perception has most often been obtained in situations where the acoustic information is degraded, as it is at a noisy party, for example. A number of authors (e.g. Miller & Niceley, 1955; Sumby & Pollack, 1954; Summerfield, 1979) have shown that seeing the speaker improves the discriminability of the speech sounds. However, Campbell also cites evidence from Reisberg, McClean, and Goldfield (1987) which suggests that comprehension of perfectly clear speech may be aided if the face can be seen. They found that speech comprehension of perceptually clear but "difficult" material (e.g. English spoken by non-native speakers, or a recited extract from Kant's *Critique of pure reason*) was better if the speaker could be seen as well as heard. This is an intriguing result, though it is not clear what information from the face was helpful in this situation, nor at what level (lexical, thematic, pragmatic) the help was gained.

Information in lip and tongue movements certainly can add nonredundant information during speech perception. Consonants which are easily confused acoustically (such as /k/ and /p/) are visually very distinctive, since /p/ involves lip closure while /k/ does not (Campbell, in press; Miller & Niceley, 1955). Summerfield (1979) demonstrated that facial speech perception depends upon much more than the mere time-varying correlation of mouth movements with acoustic variations in the amplitude of the speech signal. He compared four different "lipreading" conditions to see which aided the perception of speech in noise. In the first condition the lower half of the speaker's face was seen (i.e. normal cues for lipreading). In the second only the lips were shown, which was achieved by painting them with phosphorescent paint and filming with ultra-violet illumination. In the third, four points corresponding to the corners of the mouth and midpoints of each lip were illuminated, so that the display was the lipreading equivalent of the Johansson point-light displays of human figures. The final condition did not involve lips at all, but was a "moving ring" display in which an annulus opened and closed in synchrony with variations in the amplitude of the presented speech. He found that only the first two conditions produced better speech perception than could be achieved from the acoustic information alone. The lower half of the face produced a bigger advantage than the painted lips condition, which Summerfield suggests may be due to the absence of visible tongue movements in the latter condition. The absence of visible movements of the jaw and cheeks might also be responsible. Erber (1974) found that lipreading may be marginally easier from a $\frac{3}{4}$ view than from full-face, which may be because jaws and cheek movements are easier to see in such a display (Campbell, in press).

While movements of the lips and associated structures may aid speech perception at a lexical level, by disambiguating acoustic cues, other aspects of facial speech may help us interpret speech at a more thematic level. Brow movements may be used to add punctuation and emphasis, and brow raises may serve as question-marks (Ekman, 1979). In conversation, the listener's face may signal attention and agreement with smiles and nods, or bewilderment with a puzzled or worried expression. Before a conversation has even been initiated the eyebrow flash appears as a universal gesture of recognition and greeting (Eibl-Eibesfeldt, 1972).

Much important socio-linguistic information is thus gained, not from the lips but from the eye and brow regions of the face. Direction of gaze may itself be an important social signal (Argyle & Cook, 1976). For example, if a listener averts his or her eyes, this may signal a lack of interest in the topic or in the speaker, or embarrassment with the subject. The degree to which people engage in mutual gaze depends upon their cultural background and their degree of intimacy, but nevertheless gaze variations can give important clues which, if heeded, may smooth the course of social interaction.

FACIAL APPEARANCE AND SOCIAL ATTRIBUTIONS

We take the attractiveness of our faces very seriously, spending millions of pounds, nationally, on cosmetics and cosmetic surgery to try to enhance the better aspects of our natural appearance, or to conceal the effects of ageing. Shepherd (1981) reviews work which suggests that, at least among Western people, there is some degree of consistency in judgements of facial beauty. Consistency across time is demonstrated by Taylor and Thompson (1955) who found that line-drawn faces which were constructed to conform to Greek classical proportions (of the "golden section") were preferred to those which deviated from such proportions. Consistency between different social groups is demonstrated by Iliffe (1960) and Udry (1966). Each of these published photographs of the same small set of women in newspapers in Britain and the U.S.A. respectively. Respondents were asked to rank order the pictures according to their attractiveness. High correlations were found between the rankings given by Britons and Americans, males and females, different age groups, and different social classes.

The standards responsible for this consistency seem to be Caucasian standards. When American black and white subjects were asked to rate the attractiveness of black female faces (Martin, 1964), the ratings were highly correlated with each other, and the ratings given by the blacks correlated significantly with independent ratings of the degree to which each face showed Caucasoid features (for the whites, the correlation was positive, but not significant). However, the ratings given by American blacks did not correlate significantly (though positive) with those given by a group of Nigerian blacks, so the preferences are undoubtedly influenced by the prevailing Western cultural values. Beyond the classical "golden section" proportions, have we any idea of the features which specify this Western Caucasian "ideal"? Shepherd (1981) comments on the scarcity of studies addressing the formal properties of beauty, and the three studies he cites provide little definitive information.

It seems that facial attractiveness is a property which we can identify reliably, but cannot readily define. Yet it may have profound effects. Some provocative studies in experimental social psychology have suggested that the attractiveness of one's face may affect the kind of person you are seen to be. Dion, Berscheid, and Walster (1972) presented photographs of people who had been rated as particularly attractive, unattractive, or intermediate in appearance, and asked observers to make judgements about them. They found that the attractive people were expected to lead better lives and be happier, but were also assumed to possess more socially desirable personality traits. Dion's (1972) study was even more disturbing. She presented an account of a child's misdemeanour, along with a photograph of the child, and examined the reasons given by adults for the child's bad behaviour. The unattractive child was more likely to be seen as basically wicked (and hence acting in character), with the pretty child seen as basically good, but having an off day.

The "beautiful is good" phenomenon is not an isolated example of the attribution of unsubstantiated traits from facial information. Liggett (1974) discusses how scholars since antiquity have attempted to detail the relationships between facial features and temperament. While none of the numerous "face reading" systems have been found to have any validity, people are still quite happy to rate faces along dimensions such as honesty or intelligence, and will even judge the occupations of people whose faces they are shown (Klatzky, Martin, & Kane, 1982a; 1982b). It seems that we employ a set of stereotyped ideas about what such groups as teachers, doctors, builders, and murderers should look like and which we apply to unknown faces. Such stereotypical attributions may be entirely unreliable, but could nevertheless have important consequences. Someone with a "criminal" face may be more likely to be picked out from a line-up, or apprehended at a political demonstration, and someone with an "honest" face might command more votes at an election.

What leads us to make such judgements? Perhaps such attributions may be mediated via others which are specified physically. Berry and McArthur (1986) review work in which they have compared the attributions made to adult faces which vary in the maturity of their facial appearance. Careful work on the processes of facial growth (reviewed in Chapter 6) has described formally the effects of ageing on faces. Older faces have their features proportionately higher on the head, have smaller eyes, larger noses and so forth. Berry and McArthur's work has shown how "baby-faced" adults (sometimes produced by varying schematic faces, sometimes by variations within a sample of real adult faces) may be attributed qualities of warmth, honesty, naivety, and kindness—qualities more likely to be attributed to the young than to the old. Not all such attributions are mediated by the prior (possibly linguistic) assignment of relative age. McArthur and Apatow (1983–84) found that increasing the size of the eyes in schematic faces increased the attribution of physical weakness, submissiveness, and intellectual naivety, amongst others, but these effects were independent of differences in the perceived age and attractiveness of the faces. However, it may be that even here the attributions are mediated by other physically specified dimensions, since large eyes are characteristic of female faces (Liggett, 1974).

Some interesting recent research by Lewicki (1986a; see also 1986b) has shown how subjects can subconsciously take note of artificially manipulated relationships between appearance and personality in a way which influences their subsequent behaviour. Lewicki (1986a) showed pictures of female faces accompanied by brief case notes describing the personality of each "patient." Unknown to the subjects, all the faces with long hair were described as sharing one personality trait, while all those with short hair were described as sharing a different trait. For example, all the long-haired faces might have been described as "kind" (amongst other things which differed). When subjects were later asked to judge whether a new set of faces appeared to possess one or other of these traits, subjects' decision times were influenced by the relationship between the trait and hair length. So, subjects asked whether a new long-haired woman was kind, to use the above example, were slower to respond "yes" or "no" than subjects who had not been presented with this covariation earlier, though the experimental subjects apparently remained unaware of the earlier relationships which had been manipulated in this way.

It seems that face perception invokes attributional processes which go far beyond the information given. Shown only a face, we are prepared to judge a person's emotional state, personality traits, probable employment, and possible fate, and Lewicki's research has demonstrated how such attributional processes may be created by our unconscious assimilation of covariations between physical features and personality variables—covariations which may be perpetuated by stereotyped role portrayals in television and film.

THE RELATIONSHIP BETWEEN AFFECTIVE
PROCESSING AND IDENTIFICATION OF FACES

Having sampled, albeit briefly, aspects of nonverbal communication and attributional processes, we now return to consider the identification of faces. Can we study identification processes in isolation from other social processes involving faces? First let us consider the relationship between the perception of facial actions (as in expressions or lipreading) and identification.

The job of a system set up to recognise expression, for example, is logically quite different from that set up to recognise identity. Identification of an individual from their face requires that we classify together all instances of that person *irrespective* of their head angle, lighting, or expression. The classification of an expression, however, requires that we categorise together all similar "facial action patterns" irrespective of the faces that are making them. It seems highly unlikely that these two very different tasks could be performed on the basis of the same information extracted from a face. Our discussion of the FACS system, which seems to provide a possible account of information to which observers are sensitive when they perceive expressions, illustrates this point. It would be strange to propose that identification of an individual's face was based on analysis of the muscle configurations active at any one time—much more likely that it would be based on some consequence of the underlying bony structures (see Chapter 6). Ekman himself suggests quite clearly that the analysis of emotions and of identities each use quite different information sources. Exactly the same arguments could be used with respect to facial speech. It is highly unlikely that the information needed to distinguish different mouthed phonemes overlaps with that used to recognise individuals by their faces, beyond the obvious fact that a "mouth" is needed for both tasks.

So far, I have presented an argument on logical grounds for the dissociation of expression and facial speech perception from face recognition. In fact there is now considerable empirical evidence for this position. Consider, for example, the disorders that can follow brain injury (see Bruyer, 1986, for recent reviews). While many classically "prosopagnosic" patients (who no longer recognise familiar faces) experience difficulties with many aspects of face perception, there are some reports of patients who can interpret facial expressions correctly, while remaining unable to identify people from their faces (Bruyer et al., 1983; Shuttleworth, Syring, & Allen, 1982), and others of patients who can identify faces but have difficulty in interpreting their expressions (Kurucz & Feldmar, 1979; Kurucz, Feldman, & Werner, 1979). Studies of cerebral lateralisation also point to the independence of expression and identity analysis. Etcoff (1985) reviews studies of patients with unilateral cerebral lesions, and studies involving brief lateralised stimulus presentations to normal subjects, which suggest that the right hemisphere superiorities found for both expression analysis and identification of faces seem to be independent of one another. Turning to experimental work, several studies have found no evidence for an influence of facial familiarity or identity on expression perception. Young, McWeeny, Hay, and Ellis (1986a) found that expressions were matched no more easily if the faces viewed were familiar than if they were unfamiliar, and Bruce (1986a) found that decisions about facial expressions were not made any more quickly to familiar than unfamiliar faces. Calis and Mens (1986) found that the ability to name the perceptually "brighter" of two sequentially presented faces was not increased if both faces wore the same expression. Valentine (Note 7) found that identification of expressions, and identification of familiar faces, were differentially affected by rotation of the faces away from the vertical. Identification of faces was relatively more affected than was expression analysis, suggesting that the two judgements rely on different information extracted from the face. Finally, Bruce and Valentine (in press) found that motion made expressions relatively easy to identify from patterns of dots scattered over the surface of otherwise invisible faces, but that the identities of faces were much less readily detected from such dynamic displays (though performance was above chance even in the identification task).

Clinical dissociations have also been observed between the analysis of facial speech and that of expression and identity. Campbell, Landis, and Regard (1986) studied two patients. The first was a prosopagnosic lady who failed to recognise (or even identify the sex of) faces, and who could not interpret their expressions, but who could judge what phonemes were mouthed in photographs of faces, and was susceptible to the McGurk and MacDonald (1976) illusion (in which a seen [mouthed] phoneme which is incompatible with that which is heard can result in a perceptual "blend" of the two). The second was an alexic patient who had no problems in identifying faces or categorising their expressions, but who found it very difficult to make phonemic judgements and who was not susceptible to the McGurk and MacDonald illusion. This is a particularly intriguing dissociation, since the patients' respective difficulties in expression and facial speech analysis could be revealed even if only the lower half of the face was shown, showing that information about the configuration of the mouth is apparently analysed via separate routes for different purposes.

At present, evidence for the independent processing of identity and facial speech rests on this case study. It is to be hoped that experimental studies of normal adults will soon be conducted to supplement this evidence.

IMPLICATIONS

The evidence and arguments given here have been used by Bruce and Young (1986) to suggest that the products of facial perception include *expression codes* and *facial speech codes*, but that these are generated by routes independent of those used to recognise familiar faces (see Fig. 12,

Chapter 4). I would argue that we can study facial identification legitimately as a topic isolated from the study of at least some aspects of interpersonal communication. However, it would be over-simple to assume that all aspects of our interactive communication were irrelevant to the task of facial recognition. For example, to claim that expression or facial speech are analysed by discrete routes does not mean that *characteristic* expressions may not form part of one's memory for a particular familiar face. If someone is always smiling, the internal representation for the shapes of their facial features and their configuration will reflect this. But that does not mean that their smile must be identified *as such* for their face to be identified.

What of other "affective" aspects of face perception? Unlike expression or facial speech, the attribution of qualities such as attractiveness (and hence "goodness") and youthfulness (and hence "dependency") *are* based, like identification, on invariants of facial structure, rather than on fleeting muscular actions. There is clearly an overlap between the information sources used for some affective and identification processes. And, to my knowledge, there has been no report of any clinical or experimental dissociation between attributional and identification processes. Indeed, quite the opposite. We know that affective attributes of *unfamiliar* faces may have subtle effects on their memorability. As examples, subjects encouraged to rate the personalities of faces they view generally remember faces more accurately than subjects asked to rate their physical features (see Chapter 4 for a review of this literature), and faces which have been rated as particularly attractive, or unattractive, are more memorable than those given intermediate ratings (Shepherd & Ellis, 1973). (Unlike the effects of rated "honesty" etc. reviewed in the last chapter, this effect may not be a simple consequence of differential distinctiveness, since Shepherd [1981] argues that attractive faces are not physically distinctive.)

However, while it is clear that attributions made to unfamiliar faces have influences on their memorability, there is also evidence that memory for unfamiliar faces does dissociate, clinically, from the identification of familiar ones. Warrington and James (1967) studied a group of right-hemisphere damaged patients and found no correlation between deficits in recognising familiar faces and remembering previously unfamiliar ones. Malone, Morris, Kay, and Levin (1982) studied two prosopagnosic patients; one could match unfamiliar faces, but not recognise familiar ones, while the other showed the opposite pattern. Thus it is not clear that the kinds of judgements we make to faces with whom we are entirely unfamiliar are at all relevant to the judgements we make to our acquaintances or celebrities, and in Chapter 4, I will describe how information-processing accounts of face recognition distinguish between the derivation of *identity-*

specific semantic information about known persons, and attributions (or *visually derived* semantic judgements) made to unfamiliar ones.

To sum up, facial speech analysis and facial expression analysis probably take place via analytic routes which are independent of those used to identify faces. Attributional processes of some sorts are relevant to remembering unfamiliar faces, but recognition of familiar faces may be regarded as independent of these processes too. However, for the moment we leave open the question of the independence of the relationship between the access of visually derived and identity-specific semantic information. This question will be tackled in Chapters 4 and 5.

A final example, which is sometimes used to illustrate that there can be an intimate connection between identification and affective processing of faces, is given by *mutual* recognition—which provides an important signal for us to act upon what might otherwise be an uncertain feeling of familiarity. The opportunity for mutual recognition is something lacking from almost all the cognitive psychologist's studies of face recognition. Indeed, this fact is also missing from the police identity parade, where the witness must scrutinise a row of impassive human faces, and it is in the suspect's interest also to avoid showing any signs of anxiety, and certainly not of recognition. It seems that such "impersonal" scrutiny of live faces may actually be rather intimidating for the witness, as evidenced by Dent's (1977) demonstration that children performed more accurately with photographed than with live parades—in the latter they were reluctant to look at each face as carefully as if it were shown in a photograph. The police identity parade thus lacks an important aspect of everyday recognition, and this may make the act of recognition itself more difficult. Don Thomson (1986) recounted the anecdote of parents who failed to recognise their daughter when she was persuaded to appear in an unexpected location, and to act in the manner of a stranger. The use of photographs in much research, and the frequent use of publicly known (media) faces, precludes the study of such interactive recognition processes, and this is a factor which should be borne in mind during the remainder of this book. However, the fact that mutual recognition is an element missing from our experimental work does not mean that it cannot be accommodated by the theoretical framework developed. To anticipate, we could include mutual gaze as a contextual element influencing the recognition process in much the same way as other aspects of situational context. A person who seems familiar as a member of the family should look and greet you, and if they don't, you may re-interpret the sense of familiarity as stemming from a remarkable likeness rather than the person themselves. Conversely, a person who seems familiar from some "media" role should not look and greet, and if *they* do, this would also upset the identification process. Here again we see how our claim that the identification of faces proceeds independently of their affective processing refers to the parallel nature of the initial information-processing routes, but does not imply that the results of these different analyses are never subsequently interpreted with respect to one another. While expressions or angle of regard may be analysed by a system separate from that used to analyse the shape of the face in order to tell its sex or age, the system that *makes sense* of the observed event will probably take account of information from all these sources. A woman might interpret differently a particular stare, or smile, if it were her husband's face that wore it, rather than a stranger's.

In this chapter I have provided a very brief overview of some aspects of the social perception of faces—activities which are sometimes raised as blocks to the study of face recognition as an activity divorced from social interaction. I have acknowledged the many levels at which the face provides information which may be crucial for smooth social interaction, but maintain that, despite the complexity of the processes involving face perception, we may study the identification of familiar faces as a discrete task, proceeding independently from other activities such as the analysis of expressions, facial speech, or other attributional processes. Even where attributional processes are important, as they are in memory for unfamiliar faces, we may still study such processes as cognitive psychologists, and accommodate their effects within a coherent *information-processing* framework. In the next two chapters of the book I will describe work which has been done on the stages of perception (Chapter 3) and comprehension (Chapter 4) of faces, and the theoretical framework which has emerged to help us understand the processes of facial recognition.

3 Faces as Patterns

In Chapter 1, I suggested that problems of eyewitness reconstruction and identification of faces had highlighted our lack of knowledge about the way in which faces are represented in memory, and the processes involved in accessing these representations. In this chapter I will consider some of the psychological research which has been aimed at the theoretical question of how faces are stored and compared. We will here be concerned with relatively early visual processing of faces, and will leave aside issues of semantic representation until Chapter 4.

Tools such as Photofit and Identikit, which are used for the reconstruction of remembered faces, seem to be based upon the assumption that a face comprises a set of features which can be added and subtracted independently of one another. A face, in these terms, is simply the sum of its parts—eyes, nose, mouth, hair, and outline. Indeed Penry (1971, p. 101), the inventor of Photofit, is quite explicit on this point: "Because each facial part is the sum of its individual details and the whole face is the sum of its sections, the total assessment of it requires a careful visual addition." Does the brain somehow add up the parts of each face to form some inner mental composite? Or do we encode faces in a way which emphasises relationships between features, possibly along with details of the features themselves? This question has been one which has concerned many of those interested in face processing, and forms one of the themes in this chapter.

In this chapter I will largely be describing the work of people who, like Penry, have been content to consider the face as a two-dimensional pattern. There has typically been rather little consideration of the growth processes which constrain the 3D shapes of faces, nor of physical measurements or variations of the face on anything other than the picture plane. Thus Penry, for example, describes how faces may appear balanced or unbalanced in terms of their proportions, but these proportions are derived entirely through consideration of the face as a 2D pattern. Psychologists interested in face perception have similarly treated faces as simple patterns, varying the similarity between different faces by altering or moving facial features independently of each other and of any three-dimensional considerations (see, for example, Fig. 7). This kind of approach to face representation has also been common in the computational treatments we will meet later in the book, and for the moment I will not question the assumption.

The assumption that faces can be regarded as 2D patterns has led to a concentration on the frontal view of the face in many of the experiments we will consider, and has led many of those interested in face processing to make use of schematic faces of various kinds in their research, so that features of faces can be manipulated independently. The use of schematic or composite faces immediately entails that only the processing of unfamiliar faces can be studied, and as we will see, there is some evidence suggesting that the processing of familiar faces is weighted towards features different from those important in unfamiliar faces. A second problem is that the independent manipulation and variation of the "features" of faces in research of this kind rather begs the question of what the important features are for face perception. An additional problem is that many of the studies I review in this chapter confound *face* processing with *picture* processing—the way in which we examine two pictures in order to see whether or not they differ will not necessarily inform us of the way in which we normally examine faces in order to recognise them. These issues must be borne in mind as we review what has been learned about the processing of facial patterns.

Before embarking upon this review, I will try to clarify some of the terminology to be used. I will use the term "dimension" to encompass any single aspect of facial variation, whether this refers to a feature (length of nose could be a dimension) or to a configuration of features (distance between nose and mouth could be a dimension). I will use the term "feature" in its everyday sense (not in the technical sense of Garner [1978]) to mean a discrete component part of a face such as a nose or a chin. I will use the word "configuration" to mean the spatial inter-relationship of facial features. The same features may be rearranged to form a different configuration, but changing facial features will also change their configuration. It is not possible to manipulate features independently of their configuration—and this in itself accounts for the problems there have been researching which properties are extracted from faces.

Having specified different kinds of dimension, we may turn to consider some processing distinctions. A central question has been whether different facial features are processed independently of one another, or whether the features together interact to create some kind of indivisible configural whole or "Gestalt" which is treated as a unit. To tackle this question, people have asked whether face processing proceeds by the serial examination of different features or by the parallel examination of different features (though it may prove difficult to distinguish a serial from a parallel model where features are differentially salient). Evidence for parallel examination of different features is not in itself sufficient to demonstrate the processing of configural relationships—though it might be taken as evidence that the face is being treated as a "simple whole" (Garner, 1978). Stronger evidence for the processing of faces as configurations is revealed by studies which show that the analysis of some dimensions of the face affects the analysis of other dimensions—i.e. where there is an interaction between different dimensions of the face.

ARE FACES PROCESSED AS FEATURES OR CONFIGURATIONS?

Bradshaw and Wallace (1971) conducted an early and often-cited study aimed at addressing this question. Subjects were required to decide whether simultaneously presented pairs of Identikit faces were the same or different. "Different" pairs might differ in from one to all seven of the features from which their faces were constructed. They found that latencies were consistent with a serial, self-terminating feature comparison process. In other words, subjects inspected first the hair, then the eyes, then the nose, say, until they found a difference between the faces. If no differences were found, they responded "same." This seems such an eminently sensible strategy for subjects engaged in this task, that it is very difficult to draw any general conclusions about face processing from the results (as Bradshaw and Wallace themselves concede in their discussion). This illustrates a general problem with many experiments designed to establish how faces are processed—subjects may respond to the demands of a particular task with specific strategies which may be rather unlike their usual modes of processing.

Using drawn schematic faces in which each of five features (brows, eyes, nose, mouth, and ears) could be drawn "small," "medium," or "large," Smith and Nielsen (1970) investigated the processes underlying judgements of sameness or difference between pairs of faces separated by one, four, or ten seconds. They manipulated the number of features which were varied, and hence *relevant* to the decision, and the number of features which actually differed on "different" trials. At the shortest interval, they found that different judgements seemed to be based upon some process of feature comparison, since they were made more quickly the more features differed between the two faces; however, same judgements appeared to be based upon a more holistic comparison process, since these judgements at one second delay were not affected by the number of relevant feature dimensions. At a delay of ten seconds, however, same judgements were sensitive to the number of relevant dimensions, suggesting a switch to an independent feature comparison strategy. Thus while Smith and Nielsen's results support Bradshaw and Wallace's to some extent, they also reveal situations in which holistic processing can be observed. However, Sergent (1984) points out that the number of relevant features in this study was always confounded with the number of *irrelevant* features (since faces always had five features), making it difficult to draw firm conclusions about how the features were processed.

Matthews (1978) claimed to have demonstrated parallel processing of some facial features (specifically hairline, eyes, and chin) in same/different judgements of pairs of Identikit faces. He found equal response-times to "different" pairs where there was a change in any one of these three features, and claimed that this was due to parallel processing of the three. Sergent (1984) points out that Matthews' conclusion may be premature: Since he did not look at the patterns obtained for individual subjects, the equal latencies obtained for the three features might result from averaging over different sequential strategies. Indeed Sergent (1984) points out a general problem with all these kinds of study which attempt to distinguish serial from parallel feature processing strategies: The more features that differ between two faces, the more their configural properties will differ, so that evidence for serial processing of features will be equally consistent with the processing of configural properties.

Sergent herself (1984) also made use of same/different judgements using pairs of Photofit faces which could differ on three dimensions: eyes, chin contour, and "internal space" (whether the eyes and nose were nearer to the forehead or the chin—see Fig. 7). She argued that if each of these dimensions was processed independently of the rest (whether sequentially or in parallel), the time taken to respond "different" when more than one of the dimensions differed could never be faster than the time taken to detect a change in the most salient dimension when only a single dimension was altered. Her data showed that, for all subjects, a change in only the chin contour of the face led to faster RTs than did a change in only the eyes or internal space. However, when another dimension was changed in addition to the contour, RTs were faster still, indicating that the dimensions were being processed interactively rather than independently—values on one dimension were being influenced by values on another. Of some interest was her additional observation that, when the faces were inverted, while chin contour changes were still the most readily detected, the latency data gave no evidence for the interactive processing of different dimensions of the faces. Sergent's data thus indicate that in the processing of upright, but not inverted, faces, different dimensions of the face are responded to in an interdependent manner. However, Sergent's results may themselves depend upon the fact that one of the dimensions she used—internal space—was itself configural in nature, and indeed significant interactions were only observed between this dimension and one or

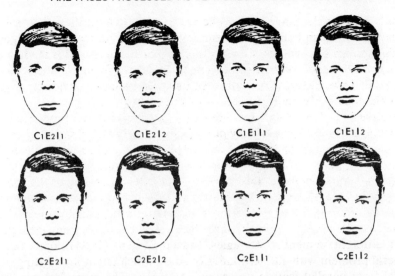

$C_1E_2I_1$ $C_1E_2I_2$ $C_1E_1I_1$ $C_1E_1I_2$

$C_2E_2I_1$ $C_2E_2I_2$ $C_2E_1I_1$ $C_2E_1I_2$

FIG. 7. The eight different faces used by Sergent (1984), made of three dimensions of two values each. The dimensions are chin contour, eyes (pupil colour and brow shape), and internal space (the relationship between the mouth and other internal features). Reproduced with permission of the author and the British Psychological Society.

both of the two other features varied. Eyes and chin contour seemed to be processed independently of each other, but interactively with internal space. Sergent (1984), like Matthews (1978), concluded that faces may be processed both as configurations and as independent parts. One way to accommodate such dual processing routes would be to suggest that an initial, coarse-scaled description of the overall configuration of the face may be used to guide the elaboration of fine-scaled detail of its various parts—a proposal which we will meet again later in this chapter.

Evidence consistent with such a proposal is found in the "face superiority effect" reported by Homa, Haver, and Schwartz (1976). They asked subjects to choose which of a small set of alternative feature forms (e.g. which of five different noses) was the one which had just been shown. They found that subjects were more accurate at this task if the feature had been shown in the context of a normal face, with eyes above nose above mouth, than if it had been shown in the context of a scrambled face, suggesting that perception of the overall facial configuration may both precede and enhance the perception of the details of features within it.

A final, recent, and compelling illustration of the power of configural processing of faces comes from Young and Hay (Note 10). They cut pictures of famous faces to produce separate top and bottom halves of each, which they then combined to form what appeared to be new

FIG. 8. The power of configural processing is demonstrated when "new" people may be created by pairing different half faces together. It is difficult to see that both the composites at the bottom contain half the face at the top. After Young and Hay (Note 10).

faces—we do not notice initially that the parts belong to familiar people. (Figure 8 illustrates this effect even with faces which will be unfamiliar to most readers: It is difficult to see that each of the composites shown contains half the face of the person above.) Young and Hay investigated this effect experimentally. First they checked that their subjects could name isolated top and bottom halves of famous faces correctly. They then explored naming latencies and accuracies for the top and bottom halves of the composite faces created by pairing the top of one face with the bottom of another. They found that subjects were much quicker at naming the separate halves when they were misaligned, than when they were correctly aligned to form a new face (as in Fig. 8). Somehow the configuration produced by the two halves produces a new identity, making it difficult to inspect each half of the face independently.

Of considerable interest was their additional observation that inverting the composite faces actually improved subjects' abilities to name the top halves of faces, compared with upright presentation. This can be explained if we assume that the configural processing which impedes recognition of the separate halves of an upright composite is less effective for inverted faces, therefore allowing the separate identities of the two halves to be revealed despite all the other difficulties associated with looking at upside-down faces. The effect thus supports the results of Sergent (1984), who found no evidence of configural processing of inverted faces.

From these studies it seems that both configural properties and information about the features present in a face are important for its perception and recognition. Reconstructive tools such as Photofit may be difficult to use, in part, because they require the witness to search through sets of alternative features in isolation from the global configuration of the face. Although a Photofit operator will always start by trying to get the overall face frame (hair and face outline) correct, features subsequently selected cannot be adjusted in subtle ways within this frame, nor can the face as a whole be altered along global dimensions. Haig (1984; 1986a; 1986b), who makes use of a sophisticated image-processing system to manipulate facial features, has shown how sensitive human observers are to tiny adjustments in the positioning of features within faces. He notes that in some cases a small movement of the mouth or eyes within a face can create the impression of a completely new individual. I will return to discuss Haig's work in more detail in the next section.

DIFFERENTIAL SALIENCE OF DIFFERENT FACIAL FEATURES

The work reviewed earlier, while suggesting a role for configural properties, does not deny a role for local details as well. And as long as witnesses tend to use conventional features in their descriptions of faces (staring eyes, big ears, crooked nose, etc.), or are required to select features from reconstructive kits, it is important to know the relative salience of the features within a face. A number of quite different research paradigms have independently pointed to the relative importance of hair, face outline, and eyes in perception and memory for faces, and the relative unimportance of the lower internal features, particularly the nose. Much of this research is very well reviewed by Shepherd, Davies, and Ellis (1981), so I will only mention some more recent studies.

Fraser and Parker (1986) report a novel technique for examining feature saliency. In their experiments, subjects were shown, in rapid sequence, each of the components of a line-drawn face. Thus they might see the outline of the face, then the eyes, then nose, then mouth. The subject's task was to detect whether or not all the components of a face were present. On some trials, one of the components was missing, and Fraser and Parker were able to compare the relative ease of detecting an absence of each of the aforementioned components. They found subjects were best at noticing the absence of the face outline, followed by eyes, then mouth, with nose the poorest.

By making use of a computer system which allowed features from one face to be stretched, compressed, deleted, or transferred to another face, Haig (1984; 1986a; 1986b) essentially confirmed these earlier findings. He found that altering the outline of the face had the greatest effect in terms of impeding recognition of the person whose face was shown. Next most important were the eyes, followed by the mouth. Changing the nose had little effect in his experiments, in line with previous research.

When Haig (1986a) used a procedure in which the key features were unspecified, but instead revealed by manipulating the nature and number of apertures through which a viewed face could be recognised, he generally confirmed the importance of the hair and eye regions in the recognition of the faces he used. However, he also noted how different individual faces seemed to be recognised by different salient features, which led him to question the whole concept of "feature saliency" lists. The fact that so many different studies produce the same overall salience effects may simply reflect average properties of the caucasian faces used.

A further point is that the relative unimportance of the nose in all these studies may be due to the difficulty of its perception in a full-face portrait. A full face probably provides the best angle to specify dimensions of eyes and mouth, but the worst for the nose, whose shape can only be perceived in an angled shot. This possible artefact does not really affect the generalisation of these results to Photofit, but we should not be justified in concluding that a witness who describes a criminal's nose is likely to be mistaken. The witness may have had a really good view of the profile, in which a distinctive nose shape could be more salient than the eyes or mouth.

A further qualification of the feature saliency results comes from the observation that the relative importance of internal (eyes, nose, and mouth) and external (hair, outline) features differs in familiar and unfamiliar face recognition. Ellis, Shepherd, and Davies (1979) showed that while internal and external features of faces were equally valid cues for recognising previously presented but otherwise unfamiliar faces, recognition of familiar faces was relatively more successful from internal rather than external features. This finding has been replicated by Endo, Takahashi, and Maruyama (1984) using Japanese faces and subjects. In a rather different face-matching paradigm, Young, Hay, McWeeny, Flude, and Ellis (1985) found that matching internal features of familiar faces was relatively more efficient than matching internal features of unfamiliar faces, in a task where matches between different views of individual faces had to be accomplished.

SPATIAL FREQUENCY ANALYSIS AND FACE PERCEPTION

Any visual pattern can be described as a distribution of light intensities in two dimensions, and can be decomposed, using the methods of Fourier analysis, into a set of underlying sine wave components of different frequencies, orientations, and amplitudes. Spatial frequency analysis has become an important tool for describing the information content in patterns, and the sensitivity of the visual system of humans and other animals. There is also a body of work which suggests that the visual system itself partitions its input into low, intermediate, and high spatial frequencies, which are carried in separate channels (Campbell & Robson, 1968; Graham & Nachmias, 1971; Wilson & Bergen, 1979). An alternative conceptualisation of the configuration/feature or global/local dichotomy in face processing is to recast these dichotomies in terms of low and high spatial frequencies (s.f.s). If higher s.f.s are removed from the spectrum of frequencies present in a picture of a face (which is what happens if the face is blurred), then the lower s.f.s remaining allow us to describe the overall configuration of the face, though the details of features are unspecified. It is the higher s.f.s which are needed to specify the details of the features.

There have been a number of claims that the information needed to recognise a face is contained largely within the low spatial frequency domain (i.e. at the level of overall configuration). Harmon's (1973) article was influential in this respect. He showed that faces which were dramatically degraded by removal of high-frequency spectral components were nonetheless fairly easy to recognise. The technique which Harmon used to filter his faces was coarse quantisation, which involves dividing the image into equal-sized square blocks, averaging the intensities within each block, and printing the results of this averaging process. The face then appears as a set of squares of varying shades of grey. If the face is divided into many thousands of such squares, then little information is lost in the quantisation process. As the number of squares per face is reduced, so the high-frequency information from the original face is progressively altered. Harmon showed that faces could still be recognised (just) from an array of only 16 × 16 squares, with at least 8 different levels of grey represented in the image.

Coarsely quantised images of the kind produced by Harmon are much easier to recognise if you blur them by squinting your eyes (see Frisby, 1979, for several examples). Why should this be? The coarse quantisation process preserves the lower spatial frequencies from the original portrait, and removes the higher ones. The quantisation process itself, however, introduces high spatial frequency "noise" to the original image. This is most noticeable as the edges of the square blocks. Harmon and Julesz (1973) investigated which of the spectral components of the noise was disrupting facial identification. Using low-pass filtered faces, they showed that adding noise from an adjacent band of the spatial frequency spectrum interfered with recognition more than adding noise from a distant, much higher band of the spectrum (analogous to that contributing to the edges of the coarsely quantised blocks). This led them to hypothesise that the quantisation process interfered with face perception by masking a "critical band" of frequencies necessary for face recognition. The quantisation process introduced noise within a spectral region adjacent to the critical band, and blurring the eyes aids face perception because it filters out these masking components. Tieger and Ganz (1979) presented evidence that it was intermediate spatial frequencies which might provide this critical band. Using faces which subtended 10° visual angle, they found that the superposition of a sinusoidal grid mask of frequency 2.2 cycles per degree disrupted recognition memory for faces more than masks of lower or higher spatial frequency.

The claim (e.g. Ginsburg, 1978; Harmon, 1973) that face recognition is dependent on particular, relatively low spatial frequency components, with higher frequencies contributing essentially redundant information, can be criticised on several counts. First, there can be no absolute spatial frequency range which is critical to face recognition, since any critical band width must be expressed in terms of cycles *per face*, rather than per degree of visual angle (Riley & Costall, 1980). As Tieger and Ganz note, a mask of about 2 cycles per degree would disrupt the features (eyes, nose etc) in the 10° faces they used. Secondly, the conclusions which are drawn from the spatial frequency work depend on the tasks which subjects are asked to do (Sergent, 1986). Thus Ginsburg (1978) used a matching task and found that low-pass filtered faces could be matched successfully against unfiltered faces, concluding that higher spatial frequencies contained information redundant for this task. Fiorentini, Maffei, and Saudini (1983) used an *identification* task, in which subjects first learned the names of several faces, and then were asked to try and identify low- and high-pass filtered versions. They found a higher identification rate with high-pass than with low-pass filtered versions. Sergent (1986) argues that a matching task may be conducted satisfactorily using only low s.f. information, while identification involves a higher level of discrimination which may require higher s.f. components. Furthermore, we must note that identification or matching *accuracy* alone is a very coarse measure. Subjects may be able to match or identify a degraded face successfully by making use of time-consuming strategies of elimination or comparison which are not needed when more spectral components are presented. Latencies should also be recorded in tasks such as these.

This brings us to a final point, which Sergent (1986) argues forcefully. In order to consider the role played by different kinds of information from faces, we must be careful to distinguish the different *uses* made of facial information (see also Bruce & Young, 1986). As I discussed at length in Chapter 2, faces are perceived in terms of their communicative and expressive content as well as serving as keys to identity. In addition, we can judge a person's sex or age even if we do not know the person viewed. Configurational information of certain kinds may subserve some of these tasks while local feature information may be required for others.

Sergent's arguments have been levelled mostly at various laterality effects which have been reported in face processing, and she also uses them to interpret patterns of apparently face-specific deficit following brain damage. Such issues are not central to this book, but I will mention just one of her own laterality studies, since it bears upon the general issue of spatial frequency processing. Sergent (1986) obtained photographs of 16 members of her department's staff, of whom half were male and half female, half were teaching staff and half support staff or students. She showed these faces to other members of her department who were all highly familiar with the people whose faces were shown. The faces were either broad-pass filtered (presenting a broad range of frequencies) or low-pass filtered, at about six cycles per face width. Three tasks were performed with the faces—naming, semantic classification (respond positively if the person is a teacher), and sex judgement. Faces were presented to the right or left of fixation, to explore processing by each cerebral hemisphere.

Sergent found that subjects were fastest on the sex judgement task and slowest on the naming task (cf. Chapter 4, especially Fig. 14). The pattern of latencies was identical for the naming and the semantic classification tasks; but naming tasks were performed more slowly throughout (cf. Young, Hay, & Ellis, 1986). Subjects responded faster to the broad-pass than to the low-pass faces on all three tasks, showing that the higher-frequency components were contributing information useful for all of the tasks explored (though the sex judgement task benefited less from the addition of these components than the other two tasks). Low-pass faces gave a right-hemisphere advantage on all three tasks, but broad-pass faces gave a left-hemisphere advantage for the naming and semantic classification tasks, showing a trend towards a right-hemisphere advantage only for the sex judgement task. While supporting Sergent's earlier thesis (e.g. Sergent, 1983) that right and left hemispheres are specialised to deal with different spatial frequencies rather than different kinds of material, her results are also consistent with her suggestion that higher spatial frequency information appears to be useful for tasks requiring identification of the faces, while low s.f.s alone may subserve tasks such as judging the sex of a face.

Sergent (1986) notes that low s.f. channels have faster integration times than higher s.f. channels, so that the kind of information which will become available most immediately is that which describes the overall facial configuration, the finer details of local features taking longer to discern. Such observations about the different time courses of different spatial frequency channels are compatible with my earlier observation (pp. 41–43) that a coarse-scale configural analysis might help refine a finer-scale feature analysis. Such progression from coarse to fine-scaled analysis has been used to increase computational efficiency in computer programs which locate and measure facial features (e.g. Craw, Ellis, & Lishman, 1987; see also Bruce & Burton, in press, for a review), and Watt (in press) describes in detail how and why the human visual system may scan from coarser to finer scales over time in order to localise visual features.

This discussion has shown how different properties of a face (configurations vs. components) may be redescribed in terms of different spatial frequency bands, and that different spatial frequencies may be more or less useful to perform different kinds of discrimination with faces. This description is useful, but requires further elaboration in terms of the relationship between early visual processes and the construction of a higher-level description of the depicted face. I will return to this issue in Chapter 6, where I deal with computational theories of face perception. For the moment, it is sufficient to note the necessity of such a higher-level description of configural properties. Spatial frequency analysis alone yields a starting point, rather than any sufficient solution to the problem of face recognition. For example, spatial frequency components are only trivially affected by inverting a face, while human face recognition is disproportionately affected.

So far in this chapter I have been considering the relative importance for facial identification of the overall configuration of a face versus its individual components. I have concluded that both contribute to face perception, though variations will be observed depending on the demands of the task in question. In the next section I turn to consider what we can learn about face perception from the study of caricature.

CARICATURE

The skilled caricature artist seems to capture, with a few pencil strokes, some definitive representation of a celebrity's face. Can we learn about the representations which subserve normal face recognition by studying cartoons? At least some cartoons are recognisable only through learned conventions and/or the operation of context (cf. Gombrich, 1972). In the context of British political news, a pair of bushy eyebrows might suffice to represent Denis Healey. However, Perkins (1975) and Perkins and Hagen (1980) argue that not all caricatures function simply by providing one or two such "tags" to identity, which have become learned symbols for the individual thus depicted. Perkins argues that many caricatures are successful at effecting recognition by functioning as "superfidelity" stimuli. They capture the essential definitive attributes of faces even more than the original faces do.

Is there any evidence for the superfidelity hypothesis? Ryan and Schwartz (1956) produced some promising results in the recognition of spatial arrangements of forms other than faces. They found that correct perception of the spatial configuration of a display required a shorter exposure duration if a "caricature" was shown than if a photograph was shown. A simple line drawing, in contrast, required longer exposure than a photograph. This experiment suggested that highlighting or exaggerating the "important" information in a picture facilitates its interpretation.

Early results obtained with faces did not support the superfidelity hypothesis. Davies et al. (1978b) found both simple and detailed line drawings of faces to form poorer representations for later recognition memory compared with photographs. This may not be a fair test for the caricature, however. The line drawing, even if detailed, may be the worst of both worlds, having lost some of the information contained in the original portrait yet not enhancing any of the information remaining (cf. Ryan & Schwartz's results). Perhaps, to quote Perkins and Hagen (1980), caricatures "speak more loudly of less." However, Hagen and Perkins (1983) obtained a result similar to Davies et al.'s using caricatures in place of line drawings. Faces which were presented and tested as caricatures were recognised less well than those presented and tested as $\frac{3}{4}$ or profile photographs. Though the hit rates did not differ much between these conditions, false positives were higher for the caricatures. When the task was to recognise a face in an altered mode (e.g. present photograph, test on caricature), performance was even worse, a result which lends little support to the original version of the superfidelity hypothesis. A similar result was recently reported by Tversky and Baratz (1985). Using photographs and caricatures of familiar (public) faces, they found that caricatures led to poorer memory than photographs, slower name-face verification times, and were rated as less "characteristic" images of the people depicted than were photographs of them. These studies by Hagen and Perkins, and Tversky and Baratz, compare caricatures with *photographs*. This comparison itself may be criticised, since a photograph must inevitably contain much more information about a face, particularly about its 3D shape, from shading and so forth, than does a line drawing of any kind.

In an unpublished student project which I supervised (Hunter, Note 4) line drawings of faces were compared with caricatures. We were primarily interested in exploring the manner in which context might operate to aid recognition of a caricature, as entailed by the tag theory. Hunter obtained simple line drawings by tracing photographs of celebrities' faces, and caricatures by tracing newspaper cartoons. Subjects had to name the faces when they were shown in a tachistoscope. The faces were preceded by various kinds of verbal phrases, analogous to cartoon punchlines. Phrases which were appropriate to the target person facilitated recognition accuracy, relative to a neutral (no phrase) condition, and phrases which were inappropriate impeded recognition. The pattern of facilitation and inhibition was the same for the cartoons and the line drawings, and for both materials the pattern was what we would expect if subjects used the punchline to help them predict which face might appear (cf. Bruce & Valentine, 1986; see Chapter 4 of this volume). However, we did not find an overall significant advantage for cartoons in this task. The line drawings led to equally fast and accurate identification. In retrospect, given the simplicity of the cartoons we chose for the study, coupled with distortions produced by tracing, this result is perhaps not too surprising. We perhaps ended up comparing rather poor caricatures with line drawings.

A much tighter study has recently been conducted by Rhodes, Brennan, and Carey (in press). They made use of a caricature generator which produced caricatures from veridical line drawings of faces by exaggerating the deviation of each face relative to a facial "norm" (see later, p. 57, and Fig. 11). Caricatures produced in this way were recognised more quickly than veridical line drawings, suggesting that caricatures can indeed be considered as superfidelity stimuli, when compared with other, potentially as informative, line drawings of faces.

Thus our conclusion may be that detailed caricatures can capture the "essence" of a face in a rather more interesting way than the tag hypothesis suggests. A caricature may not be *as good* a representation of a celebrity's face as a high quality *photograph*, but it is still, often, a good representation. And, as Perkins (1975) illustrates, *bad* caricatures are not "caricatures" at all. Goldman and Hagen (1978) present a detailed formal analysis of the cartoons of Richard Nixon produced by a large number of different artists. They compared measurements of various proportions such as nose length:head length obtained from photographs of Nixon, with the same ratios measured in cartoons of him. Although different artists varied in the *amount* of distortion they imposed on these ratios, the artists agreed closely in terms of which ratios they distorted the most and which they distorted the least. Thus attributes of Nixon's face which one artist tended to exaggerate a lot were the same as those that another exaggerated a lot, and those attributes which one artist left relatively untouched were the same as those that another left alone. This formal analysis largely supported an earlier analysis by Perkins (1975), which was based on a much smaller sample of caricatures and only informal inspection of Nixon's actual facial attributes. Perkins found that the artists he studied agreed fairly closely on the attributes of Nixon's face which they highlighted, with all exaggerating his nose, jowls, hairline, and box chin.

In his formal definition of caricature, Perkins (1975) suggests that: "a caricature is a symbol that exaggerates measurements relative to individuating norms." An "individuating norm" is any measure which varies from one individual to another. Thus nose length forms an individuating norm, whereas number of eyes does not. Someone who has a long nose, relative to most other noses, can be caricatured with an extremely long nose. Thus the trends within the face are highlighted by a caricature. This is not quite enough, however, since the exaggeration process must preserve the relationships between the different features or other attributes. Thus a drawing of a typical face with the addition of a long nose would not serve as a caricature of Nixon (see Fig. 9). But the attributes of nose, jowls, hairline, and box chin seem to be those which are "fairly necessary," and will serve to define Nixon's face, provided that values on other attributes or dimensions (such as overall head shape or fatness) do not depart too radically from appropriate ones. Caricature thus provides us with a rather

FIG. 9. The figure at the left shows a veridical line drawing of ex-President Nixon, obtained by tracing a photograph of him. The next panel shows a caricature, which proves more recognisable. The final panel shows a "bad" caricature in which some of Nixon's distinctive features are shown in relationship to the wrong underlying facial structure. Drawings by Perkins (1975), reproduced with permission.

different line of evidence for the role of the overall configuration, rather than individual features, in recognition.

It is interesting to note that cartoonists often report a preference for showing a $\frac{3}{4}$ view rather than full face or profile. Of the 38 caricatures of Nixon studied by Perkins, 27 were $\frac{3}{4}$ views. We will return to the possible importance of this in Chapter 5, and again in Chapter 6, when we consider computational approaches to the retrieval of face shape. Cartoonists also report difficulty in caricaturing an "ordinary" face. Gerald Ford apparently posed problems in this respect, and political cartoonists faced with the ordinary may perhaps be more likely to resort to a tag (such as Wilson's pipe) to support their drawing, or to depict a characteristic expression.

Caricatures are effective because they exaggerate the trends in a face—trends of attribute values relative to one another (a large nose is not a large nose in a large head), and relative to the population of faces generally. Unfortunately, the study of "natural" (i.e. artists') caricatures can be no more than suggestive about theories of face representation at present, since the published studies have been confined to images of a single figure (such as Nixon). For example, Perkins observed that other apparently distinctive features of Nixon, such as his baggy eyes and eyebrow shape, were not incorporated reliably into cartoons of him. Is this because they do not serve to individuate Nixon, because they are not generally useful for recognition purposes, or because different artists see each others' work and adopt a particular set of conventions for depicting particular faces? A study of a large number of caricatures of a range of different celebrities might be revealing. The study of artificial generation of caricatures by Brennan (1985) is potentially very informative here, and I will return to consider this work later in this chapter. In the next section I will first consider further independent evidence for the suggestion that faces may be represented in terms of their deviations from the norm.

DISTINCTIVENESS

Cartoonists reputedly have a difficult time caricaturing an ordinary-looking face. Perkins' claim that a caricature exaggerates trends in the face—trends along individuating dimensions—may be rephrased in terms of distinctiveness. A cartoonist exaggerates the distinctive attributes of the face while preserving the typical ones. The fact that cartoons remain recognisable despite such distortions in their absolute values should be accommodated by a theory of facial representation.

Our observations about caricature might be accommodated by a theory of face recognition in which faces were stored, not as a metric of actual feature measures, but in terms of their deviations from the average or typical face. While a cartoon would not preserve accurately the degrees of deviation, it would preserve their pattern. Is there any evidence that deviations from the "norm" form the basis for everyday face recognition?

I have already mentioned work (Chapter 1) in which it was shown that distinctive faces are better retained in recognition memory tasks than are typical faces (Bartlett, Hurrey, & Thorley, 1984; Cohen & Carr, 1975; Going & Read, 1974; Light et al., 1979; Winograd, 1981). Is this an effect which occurs only in the remembering of unfamiliar faces? Or can we observe effects of distinctiveness even in our everyday recognition of familiar ones? Tim Valentine, working with me in Nottingham, has recently conducted a number of experiments on effects of distinctiveness in the recognition of highly familiar faces.

In one study (Valentine & Bruce, 1986b), the relative distinctiveness of the faces of a number of members of our academic staff was rated by asking students to pick out the face which would be "easiest to spot in a crowd," and repeating this procedure until all the faces had been removed. Students who were familiar with the faces were tested as well as some who were unfamiliar, and a high correlation was found between the distinctiveness ratings obtained by these two groups. These faces were then intermixed with an equal number of unfamiliar faces and presented to students who knew the academic staff faces, who were asked to decide, as quickly as possible, whether each face was familiar or not. We found that distinctiveness was negatively correlated with the time taken to decide that each face was familiar. The *more* distinctive the face, the *shorter* the decision time. It was possible to obtain, from the same students, data about the relative familiarity of these staff faces. This also correlated negatively with decision time (the more familiar faces were responded to more quickly), but distinctiveness and familiarity were not correlated with one another, and the correlations of each of these dimensions with decision time remained very similar if the other dimension was partialled out.

This preliminary study, using correlational techniques, suggested that even for highly familiar faces, distinctiveness is a factor affecting ease of recognition. In subsequent experiments (Valentine & Bruce, 1986c; Valentine, Note 7) this finding was confirmed and extended. Using the faces of celebrities, again rated for distinctiveness, two separate groups of "distinctive" and "typical" faces were obtained. None of the faces was bearded or wore glasses. Distinctive faces included Denis Healey, and typical faces, David Steel. In a familiarity decision task, distinctive faces were recognised more quickly than typical faces, confirming the earlier findings.

If such an effect is due to some explicit or implicit comparison with a facial "schema" (Goldstein & Chance, 1980) or "prototype" (Light et al., 1979), then distinctive faces should be at a *disadvantage* when the task is changed to that of making decisions about whether each item is a *face* or not, since typical faces should resemble the prototypical face more closely than distinctive faces. In further experiments, distinctive and typical faces were intermixed with jumbled faces (in which eyes, nose, and mouth were rearranged, see Fig. 10), and subjects had to respond positively if each item was a "face" and negatively if it was a jumbled face. All the items had lines drawn on them so that the task could only be performed by examining the configuration of eyes, nose, and mouth. As predicted by the prototype theory, distinctive faces were now slower to categorise as faces than were typical ones.

This research thus shows that the relationship between the structure of an individual's face, and some average of all faces typically encountered in a culture, has reliable effects on how easily the face can be perceived. When discussing caricature, we noted that Perkins suggested that these were constructed by exaggerating the trends in a face—again as compared with average values. Perhaps we should consider the representation of faces in terms of patterns of deviation from an underlying norm, or average.

It is in this context that Brennan's (1985) caricature generator obtains its significance. Her technique works as follows (see also Dewdney, 1986, for a description). Full-face photographs are represented as 186 key points obtained from the outline of the face, hairline, and internal facial features. These points can be joined up to form a line drawing of the face (see Fig. 11). The co-ordinates of these points are scaled so that the left and right pupils are given constant co-ordinate values—thus all faces can be scaled to coincide on these key points, so that meaningful comparisons can be made between the point representations of one face and another. Brennan

FIG. 10. An example of a "face" and a "jumbled face" as used in face classification tasks by Valentine and Bruce (1986c).

FIG. 11. The face shown on the left is a true outline drawing of Ronald Reagan's face, obtained by joining up points traced from an original photograph. The face on the right is a computer-generated caricature of Reagan, made by exaggerating the positions of the points located in the original face, in proportion to their deviation from the corresponding points of a typical face (obtained from averaging across lots of faces). The figures were produced by Susan Brennan, and are reproduced with permission.

encodes a number of faces in this way and takes the average of the co-ordinates for each of the key points to produce a representation of a face "norm." A face whose caricature is required is then represented in terms of its co-ordinate points, and these are compared with the average values. To produce a caricature, differences between the target face values and the average face values are exaggerated by multiplication. The greater the value of the multiplication parameter, the greater the degree of distortion—and at extreme values the line-drawn face ceases to look like a face at all. At less extreme values, extremely effective caricatures result from the redrawing of the target face from the exaggerated control points, as shown in Fig. 11.

Rather than thinking of each face as represented by 186 pairs of co-ordinate values, Brennan (1985) conceives of each face as a single point in a multidimensional space—where each *dimension* in the space is the x or y co-ordinate value of a particular point. In such a face "space," dissimilar faces lie far apart, and similar faces will lie close together (cf. Goldstein, Harmon, & Lesk, 1971). Indeed, a large number of faces will be represented as a cluster around their "average" values, with the more distinctive faces lying at the fringes of such a cluster. Valentine (Note 7) has proposed a very similar idea in order to provide a conceptual framework for his experimental effects of distinctiveness, but for him, the "dimensions" of the space are much more abstract parameters derived from faces,

R.F.—E

such as variations in particular facial features, or more global variations such as age. A face is again conceived of as represented as a "point" in this multidimensional space. The deviation of any individual face from the prototype or average face is given by the vector between the co-ordinates of the individual face and the co-ordinates of the prototype. In these terms, a caricature could provide a good representation of a particular individual's face if it preserved the direction of this vector.

Valentine (Note 7) has used this multidimensional space framework to clarify the way in which face recognition and face classification tasks should be affected by distinctiveness, inversion, and the race of the presented faces. For example, Goldstein and Chance (1980) implied that inverted faces might be hard to recognise because the learned face "schema" or prototype could not be accessed during encoding. This position leads to the prediction that distinctiveness effects should not be found with inverted faces. Valentine (Note 7) suggests, instead, that inverted faces are difficult because their dimensions are *difficult* to encode, which adds uncertainty or noise to their representation in multidimensional space, but that effects of distinctiveness should still be found with inverted faces. He has demonstrated that inverted distinctive faces are more difficult to classify as faces than inverted typical faces, and that effects of inversion and distinctiveness are additive in this task, consistent with this prediction.

Unlike face classification, recognition of the familiarity of individual faces requires that different points in face space be distinguished from one another. The greater the density of points in the neighbourhood, the harder this will be. This describes the effect of distinctiveness in familiarity judgement, but leads to the prediction that inverting the faces should produce an interaction with distinctiveness in a familiarity judgement task. This prediction is currently being tested.

Other-race faces form a rather interesting class of stimuli here. Shepherd (1981) reviews evidence which suggests that the dimensions of facial variation to which it is appropriate to attend for discrimination purposes differ depending on the race of the faces. Let us suggest, like Shepherd, that subjects viewing other-race faces may inappropriately encode them along the dimensions of variation which are familiar from faces of their own race. Then while the representation of any particular other-race face will deviate to a large extent from the face prototype values learned from own-race faces, a set of other-race faces will form a cluster of points with very similar co-ordinates, and hence a group of other-race faces should behave like a group of "typical" faces, being difficult to recognise upright, and particularly hard to recognise when inverted. Using a recognition memory paradigm with unfamiliar black and white faces, we have already confirmed this predition (Valentine & Bruce, 1986a). Other-race faces should, however, behave like distinctive faces in a face classification task, and be relatively difficult to categorise as faces. Tim Valentine has recently demonstrated this.

This kind of analysis can allow us to explain how a less familiar group of faces (those of another race) can be more disrupted by inversion, while maintaining at the same time that effects of inversion arise as a consequence of familiarity with faces as a class. Our disproportionate experience with upright faces of our own race leads to our facility at encoding them along particular dimensions. These dimensions may include configural properties, and it may be these which are particularly hard to extract from inverted faces. This analysis is also compatible with Diamond and Carey's (1986) observation that disproportionate effects of inversion can arise given expertise with other classes of shapes where subtle differences in configuration are likely to be important for discrimination.

It is interesting that such similar ideas have evolved, quite independently, from attempts to synthesise caricatures, and to explain experimental effects using normal photographs. One thing clearly lacking, however, is a formal scheme for deciding what the dimensions of facial variation should be. It seems unlikely that the human brain computes the values of particular key points of the kind used in Brennan's scheme, and much more likely that parameters specifying both local features and global configurational variations are the components of our representations for face recognition. Whatever the dimensions of facial variation, these multi-dimensional space accounts suggest that effects of facial "prototypes" somehow emerge from the encoding and storage of large numbers of faces with similar visual properties. In Chapter 5 we will consider how recent work on distributed memory models may be able to accommodate these ideas.

We will defer further discussion of the "front end" of face recognition—the construction of visual representations—until later, in Chapters 4 and 6. For the moment, note that the available evidence has revealed differences in the relative salience of different features of a face, but also emphasised that configural properties, and relationships with the "average" face, seem to play an important role in facial representation. Reconstructive kits such as Photofit do not readily capture these aspects of our representation of faces, and in Chapter 6 I will return to consider the implications of these findings for such forensic aids. It is not only the inventor of Photofit who lacks insight into the way in which we represent faces. As I mentioned in Chapter 1, a marked *dissimilarity* was noted between the face of Mr. Virag and that of Mr. Payen, for whom Mr. Virag was apparently mistaken by a number of independent witnesses. However, the face of Mr. Virag seems to share many distinctive features (thin lips, fine pointed nose, etc.) with that of Mr. Payen (see Devlin, 1976, p. 66). Given hats, which were worn in the original incident and in the identification parades, the two men seem to share a strong resemblance, despite some obvious differences in certain details such as their ears. It would be interesting to make a more formal examination of the nature of this apparent resemblance, which led to Mr. Virag's wrongful conviction.

In the next chapter, I move on from this discussion of the nature of representations which may be used to recognise faces, to discuss how such visual representations access the semantic information which specifies individual identity.

4

Semantic Coding of Faces

In the last chapter I addressed the question of what information is derived from faces that allows us to distinguish between them. I concluded that configural and local feature information were both important, and that faces might be represented in a way which captured the deviation of an individual face from some representation of the average or prototype of all encountered faces. In this chapter, I will refer to the end product of this visual encoding of a face as a "structural code" for the face. Whatever the details of the visual representation of faces (an issue I return to later in this chapter and in Chapter 6), it has been assumed, implicitly, that recognition of the familiarity of an individual face results from matching a structural code derived from it with a stored structural code which characterises some known individual's face. Any such matching process can, however, only form a first stage in the recognition of a face. As I argued in Chapter 1, a theory of face recognition must explain how we *interpret* the apparent familiarity of faces that we see. A sense of familiarity *alone* is not sufficient to guide our social activities, nor is it a satisfactory state to remain in ("who is that man? . . . where have I seen him before? . . . why does he seem familiar?"). Face *recognition* usually entails face *identification*. We see a face and know that it is Fred or Irene, or the butcher, or the lady-who-lives-at-number-3. The witness asked to identify a suspect from an identity parade must identify a person as their assailant, or the robber, or whatever. This is why exposure to photographs prior to a parade should invalidate that parade, since a mere sense of familiarity will be difficult or impossible to interpret.

The act of face recognition therefore requires that we somehow get from a visual pattern (a face) to a semantic level of representation where the identity of the person is specified. I will refer to the products of this semantic level as *identity-specific semantic codes*. For highly familiar faces, identity-specific semantic codes may encompass many "facts" about the person (their occupation, marital status, age, address, and so forth). A familiar person can also (usually) be named, though, as I will explain later, there are good reasons for treating the *name* as a code distinct from identity-specific semantics. For less familiar faces, their identity may be some memory of where they are usually encountered (e.g. "the lady who works in the sweet shop"). For the unfamiliar faces shown in laboratory experiments, successful recognition involves correctly recalling the context in which they were encountered ("that face was presented in the list I saw earlier"). The extent to which such episodic contextual associations may in practice be distinguished from identity-specific semantic information will be addressed later. For the moment, the important point is that whether we are talking about "episodic" recognition memory for previously unfamiliar faces, or the identification of highly familiar ones, complete recognition requires that a sense of familiarity be supplemented by further contextual or semantic information. In this chapter I will consider some of the processes which may be involved in attaining the complete recognition of faces, both in episodic recognition memory for unfamiliar faces, and in the recognition of highly familiar faces. Initially, these two areas will be considered separately, as they have given rise to rather different kinds of theoretical account (just as theories of verbal episodic memory have tended to be quite distinct from those of word recognition). Later in this chapter, and in subsequent ones, I will enquire whether these two areas can be given a unified theoretical treatment.

During the course of the chapter, it will be found useful to distinguish a number of further information "codes" which may result from processing faces. So far in this chapter I have already mentioned structural codes, which describe the distinguishing aspects of individual facial structure, identity-specific semantic codes, and names. At the level of visual representations, structural codes for faces may be distinguished from what I have termed *pictorial codes* (Bruce, 1982; 1983; Bruce & Young, 1986), which are representations of particular pictures of faces. Every different picture of a particular individual's face will give rise to a different pictorial code, but should give rise to the same structural codes (or at least similar enough to mediate consistent recognition). At the level of semantic representations, as I noted in Chapter 2, there is a distinction between identity-specific semantic codes, and what Bruce and Young (1986) termed *visually derived semantic codes*. Visually derived semantic codes result from attributions made on the basis of what the face looks like. We might decide that a face looks female, even though we know it is male. In this chapter I will describe how each of these different codes may be derived when we perceive faces, and the role each may play in our acts of recognition.

At several points in this chapter, I will explore the utility of borrowing theoretical concepts from the huge literature on verbal memory and reading in an attempt to account for interpretation and memory for faces. Despite the special social functions subserved by faces, their identification may involve similar principles to those involved in the identification of other kinds of visual pattern. And, whatever the utility of comparisons between the identification of faces, and the identification of other objects or words, such analogies do not deny that other aspects of face processing may be unique to faces. It may be that "unique" processes are involved, for example, in the analysis of facial expressions, or in the derivation of visual representations suitable for recognition processes (see Chapter 6).

The act of identifying a familiar face can be compared quite naturally with that of understanding a word—readers need to know more than that the word has been seen before; they must know what it means. A person viewing a photograph of Ronald Reagan, or the words "RONALD REAGAN," must in both instances get from the visual pattern to a semantic level to do with America, presidents, and Republicanism. In both cases the shapes of the pattern are not themselves sufficient to determine this semantic interpretation. (A face like Reagan's could be that of a bus-driver, bank manager, or ageing sportsman.) There is essentially arbitrary relationship between the surface form of a face, or a name, and its identity-specific semantics. This analogy between face and word interpretation does not, of course, imply that all aspects of interpretation are the same for faces and words. The perceiver may notice that the face (but not the name) of Reagan is smiling, or looks old, or may notice that the words (but not the face) are written in a distinctive handwriting. However, these are semantic levels which are independent of that to do with identity. Later in this chapter I will argue, as I have elsewhere, that useful comparisons can be made between the access of identity-specific semantics from faces and words (more especially, names).

What of episodic recognition memory? Can comparisons be made here between memory for faces and words? This is the topic I begin with, by considering how context effects may influence the recognition of these very different kinds of item. The analogy here is complicated by the fact that words used in recognition memory experiments are always familiar (since they are in the subject's vocabulary), and so the subject's task is always to remember the context in which a word was last seen. For faces of unfamiliar people, which are typically the materials used in recognition memory experiments, any sense of familiarity may be used to reach a decision that an item is a target, rather than a distractor. The task demands of episodic recognition memory for words are thus somewhat different from those for previously unfamiliar faces, and a more valid comparison might be between recognition memory for nonsense words and unfamiliar faces, or between words and familiar faces. However, although this argument might lead us to predict that contextual reinstatement should be relatively unimportant for facial compared with verbal recognition memory (since face targets may be recognised on the basis of familiarity alone), in fact we find that contextual effects are rather more readily demonstrated for faces than for words in such tasks.

CONTEXT EFFECTS IN FACE RECOGNITION MEMORY

In tasks of verbal *recall* there have been numerous demonstrations of beneficial effects of reinstating acquisition context at time of test. As examples, words studied in one room are better recalled in the same than in a different room (Smith, 1979), and words studied by divers underwater are better recalled underwater than on land, and vice versa (Godden & Baddeley, 1975). Such effects of the environmental context at test do not, however, extend to recognition memory for words. Thus Godden and Baddeley (1980) found no effect of reinstating the underwater or land context when the task was changed to one of discriminating previously presented words from new distractor items.

However, effects of contextual reinstatement can be observed in recognition memory for words where the context influences the semantic interpretation of the word (e.g. Light & Carter-Sobell, 1970; Tulving & Thomson, 1971). The word JAM studied in the context STRAWBERRY will be less well recognised at test if paired with the word TRAFFIC, than if the encoding context is reinstated. Baddeley and Woodhead (1982) argue for a distinction between *independent* and *interactive* contexts. The environmental context in which a word is seen functions independently. While it might provide an additional retrieval cue in a recall test, it will be of no beneficial effect in a recognition test, where retrieval processes are minimised. Only interactive contexts, which change the nature of the item's encoding, will influence recognition memory performance.

When we turn to consider the effects of contextual reinstatement on face recognition, we find beneficial effects of contexts which, at first glance, seem more analogous to the environmental (and hence, supposedly "independent") contexts in verbal memory. Although Bower and Karlin (1974) failed to find any beneficial effect of testing faces alongside the same partner faces with which they had been paired at presentation, all subsequent experiments of this kind have found positive effects. Watkins, Ho, and Tulving (1976) and Winograd and Rivers-Bulkeley (1977) found, unlike Bower and Karlin, that faces were better recognised if partners were the same at test compared with when they were changed. Klee, Leseaux, Malai, and Tiberghien (1982) found effects of changing the pictured background context against which faces were presented at study and test, and similar effects have been found by Thomson, Robertson, and Vogt (1982) and Davies and Milne (1982). This last study is important in showing an effect of contextual change for faces whose pose and expression were changed between study and test, a situation which should more adequately test "facial" as opposed to "pictorial" memory.

In more naturalistic simulated studies of eyewitnessing, there have been claims that returning subjects to the room in which a target person was originally observed can lead to better recognition of that person from a line-up (Wagstaff, Note 8), or that encouraging the mental reinstatement of the environmental and emotional conditions in which an incident was originally viewed can have similar beneficial effects on person recognition (Malpass & Devine, 1981). Positive effects of both physical and mental reinstatement of context have also been shown in Photofit construction, a task which contains elements of recall as well as recognition (Davies & Milne, 1985). Davies (1986) reviews these and other studies which have shown positive effects of physical reinstatement of context and/or guided memory techniques. However, Graham Davies (personal communication) has also suggested that many failures to find positive effects of this kind on simulated witness recognition performance may go unreported. Certainly Amina Memon (Note 5), working with me in Nottingham, was unable to show any effects on recognition accuracy of returning "witnesses" to the room in which an incident took place, or of guided memory techniques. She did, however, replicate effects of pictured background context (cf. Klee et al., 1982; Davies & Milne, 1982, etc.) in tasks of remembering photographs of faces.

It thus appears that while there are clear effects of reinstating the background context (accompanying face, pictured background scene, and so forth) presented with a pictured face in a laboratory task of face recognition, the effects of similar contextual cues in more naturalistic witnessing episodes are less clearcut. It is not really helpful here to suggest that a pictured background context may be "interactive" while the room in which an episode occurs is "independent." The concepts become essentially circular. Instead, more consideration must be given to the encoding processes elicited by the tasks. I will discuss this in detail after considering the way in which contextual effects may be influenced by encoding strategies. First I must digress to consider how manipulation of encoding strategies per se may affect the accuracy of episodic face recognition.

LEVELS OF PROCESSING

One of the most influential theories of human memory to emerge in recent years was Craik and Lockhart's (1972) "levels of processing" framework. Their claim was that memory was a by-product of perceptual processing, and that the more deeply (in semantic terms) an item had been processed, the better would be its subsequent retention. Items (usually words) which had been processed only at a surface (sensory) level would be less well retained than those which had been processed to a deep (semantic) level. At a rigorous theoretical level, Craik and Lockhart's framework was riddled with problems (e.g. see Baddeley, 1978). However, at an operational level, some principle of encoding "depth" or "elaboration" has been found to hold good in a wide range of experiments using verbal materials, including recognition memory tasks (Craik, 1983, reviews this literature).

Bower and Karlin (1974) were the first to report an apparent effect of depth of processing in a face recognition task. In an incidental learning test, subjects who had judged the sex of each face at presentation subsequently recognised far fewer than those who had rated each in terms of its apparent intelligence. While this result might be an artefact of the relative time needed to judge sex and intelligence respectively, the effect has been replicated in other studies (e.g. Patterson & Baddeley, 1977; Winograd, 1976). Patterson and Baddeley's subjects rated each face either in terms of a series of physical features, or in terms of a series of personality traits. In this situation, too, the semantic orienting task (personality traits) led to better recognition memory performance than did the physical orienting task.

The apparently beneficial effect of semantic processing on facial recognition is important theoretically, extending the domain in which effects of depth/elaboration apply; it is also of practical importance. Patterson and Baddeley's results suggest that trying to form an overall impression of a person's character from their face may lead to better memory than concentrating on the details of each physical feature. Such a suggestion is in direct contradiction to the advice offered by Penry (1971) in his book on remembering faces. He suggests that witnesses should carefully inspect and label each visual feature in an analytic way.

However, Winograd (1978) has suggested that the apparent advantage for "trait" orienting tasks might have more to do with the number of physical features sampled than with the semantic nature of the task. He found that subjects asked to rate the most distinctive feature of a face performed equivalently to those asked to rate personality traits, and claimed that, under such conditions, both groups of subjects were required to analyse the whole face. A further setback for a simple "levels" interpretation of the "trait" effect comes from the demonstration that orientation to the physical features of a face leads to better memory performance when this is tested through reconstruction of the face with Identikit (Wells & Hryciw, 1984). Thus it appears that encoding instructions do not have a simple effect upon the durability of the memory trace; rather it is the relationship between encoding activity and the nature of the retrieval test which is crucial. Such an observation makes it impossible to recommend that people should view faces in a particular way in order to remember them—it depends how their memories will be tested.

The notion of simple depth of processing thus appears unsuccessful as a general principle in face perception and memory. Nevertheless, as we will see, variations in encoding instructions in experiments involving contextual change have revealed important clues about the manner in which the latter may operate. This leads us to consider more carefully the nature of the semantic codes that trait orienting instructions actually affect. When applied to verbal memory, the main weakness of the levels of processing theory was its proposal of a simple hierarchy of levels from the sensory to the semantic. For faces, it is important that we distinguish the different uses to which the information from a face can be put (cf. Wells & Hryciw, 1984), which may require that we specify different kinds of physical feature information and certainly many kinds of semantic interpretation. The "semantic" orienting tasks used by Bower and Karlin (1974), Patterson and Baddeley (1977), and Winograd (1978) did not involve forming or elaborating identity-specific semantic information, as defined earlier, but required that subjects make semantic impressions based upon the actual visual pattern of each face. The faces they rated as low in intelligence might, in actuality, have belonged to professors, and those rated as friendly might belong to misanthropes. As discussed earlier and in Chapter 2, rating a face according to its apparent sex, intelligence, occupation, or whatever involves constructing what Bruce and Young (1986) have labelled *visually derived* semantic codes. The distinction between identity-specific and visually derived semantic information is an important one when we consider the relationship between encoding activity and context effects.

ENCODING ACTIVITY AND CONTEXT EFFECTS

Daw and Parkin (1981) were the first to demonstrate that different encoding activities had different consequences for the encoding of pictured background context. They found that subjects encouraged to rate faces in terms of personality judgements were very much better able to recall the context against which each face had been shown than were subjects who rated faces in terms of their physical features. In Nottingham, Amina Memon and myself (Memon & Bruce, 1983) reasoned that if "trait" judgements led to better retention of context, then subjects making trait judgements should be more impaired than those rating physical features when the context was changed between study and test. A control group was included who were told that their memory would be tested (the trait and feature groups were tested on incidental memory), but whose encoding strategies were not deliberately manipulated. As predicted, we found that subjects who had rated each face according to its most distinctive feature were unaffected by change in background context, while those asked to give a distinctive personality description were highly affected when the pictured background was changed from, say, a bank to a restaurant. The control group (intentional learning) performed in a way similar to the "trait" group. Moreover, the effects of contextual change do not appear to be purely pictorial. Like Klee et al. (1982), we found that changing the context to a different picture of the same semantic type (one restaurant to another) impaired recognition memory less than a change to a different semantic type.

Beales and Parkin (1984) obtained results similar to our own. Subjects rating personality traits were more impaired by a change in background context between study and test than were subjects who rated physical features. However, Beales and Parkin found that these subjects also showed some influences of contextual change, unlike Memon and Bruce (1983), but consistent with other results obtained by Memon (Note 5). Beales and Parkin's experiment is important, since its design controls for the possibility of response bias effects. All the contexts at test were "old" ones; what changed was whether they appeared with the same or with different faces.

These results show that subjects will be more likely to retain details of the background context (and hence be more impaired if this is subsequently altered) if required to assess the personalities of the people whose faces they study, than if asked to rate their physical features. Clearly there are rather subtle interactions between encoding activities and contextual manipulations in recognition memory for faces.

What theoretical explanation can we offer for such effects? Face recognition memory generally, and context effects in particular, are not easily accommodated within the kind of two-stage model of recognition memory developed within verbal memory (e.g. Juola, Fischler, Wood, & Atkinson, 1971; Mandler, 1980). In Mandler's model, for example, an initial "familiarity judgement" stage is distinguished from a subsequent stage of contextual "retrieval." The judgement of familiarity in this model must be based upon assessment of incremental rather than absolute familiarity levels, in order to explain why recognition memory is better for low- than for high-frequency words. The idea of "increments" in familiarity makes little sense when applied to recognition memory for unfamiliar faces, nor would such an account explain why recognition memory for familiar faces is so much better than for unfamiliar ones (e.g. Bruce, 1982)—in fact it should predict the opposite. Furthermore, such models do not address questions about the circumstances under which contextual information will be encoded in the first place.

We can instead explain contextual effects in face recognition memory if we think carefully about the nature of the information codes which may be derived from faces in experiments such as these, and make some fairly simple assumptions about the way such codes may be used in tests of recognition memory. For example, I explained these contextual effects (Bruce, Note 2; see also Memon & Bruce, 1985) as resulting from the level of visually derived semantic codes. A person dressed smartly and standing in front of a bank may be more likely to be rated as "honest," "intelligent," or "introverted" than the same person wearing jeans at a football ground. The entire context is likely to be relevant to the impression formation process, but irrelevant to the judgement of physical features (here it is the population of faces as a whole which is important). Thus just as the contextual word STRAWBERRY will influence the semantic interpretation of the word JAM, so will the background context influence the semantic interpretation of the person seen within it.

This account can explain the observed influences of contextual change on recognition memory accuracy if we apply a variation of Tulving's "encoding specificity" principle to faces (cf. Bruce, 1982; 1983; Memon & Bruce, 1985). Assume that recognition memory will be improved the more "codes" at test there are which match those constructed at presentation. The codes likely to be important in recognition memory for unfamiliar faces are both visual and semantic. At the visual level, I suggested earlier a distinction between "pictorial" and "structural" visual codes (cf. Bruce, 1982; 1983; Bruce & Young, 1986). Pictorial codes represent the surface form of the picture while structural codes capture aspects of the face which remain invariant across different views. In addition, the visual pattern of each face may be used to derive semantic information about age, sex, apparent personality, occupation, and so forth (visually derived semantic codes). Where a face is tested in the same view and against the same background as at study, pictorial, structural, and visually derived semantic codes will all match at test. Changing the view of a face between presentation and test would reduce recognition accuracy, since pictorial codes will not now match (Bruce, 1982; Memon, Note 5). Changing the background context in which a face appears may mean that the visually derived semantic codes formed at test do not match those formed at presentation, thus reducing recognition accuracy from that observed when context remains unchanged. Davies and Milne (1982) found additive effects of pose and context change in their study, consistent with independent effects at the level of pictorial and semantic codes. Instructing subjects to form personality impressions from faces (the "trait" condition) is likely to maximise visually derived semantic coding, and hence produce more sensitivity to the effects of context change. However, trait instructions will not necessarily lead to superior performance overall compared with feature analytic instructions (cf. Winograd, 1978). If the nature of the physical feature task encourages an elaborated pictorial or structural code, then such a task could lead to good recognition memory performance on this basis. And where the nature of the memory task specifically requires access to the pictorial or structural coding level, as in Wells and Hryciw's use of recall via Identikit, physical feature instructions may give superior performance.

Why, in these terms, are there sometimes failures to demonstrate contextual reinstatement effects in situations involving the witnessing of more realistic events (e.g. Memon, Note 5)? For example, in one experiment, Memon found no advantage when she tested face recognition via a photo line-up in the same room in which the target person had been seen, compared with testing in a quite different room. Since both rooms were in the same (university Psychology department) environment, from the point of view of her subjects (who were visiting high school students) the contexts may not have been sufficiently different to influence selectively any semantic coding of the target person. In retrospect, it might have been more interesting to manipulate the context at test in terms of the semantic coding which subjects might have applied in the original incident, where the target person appeared as a photographer who had mistakenly entered the office thinking he was to photograph the subjects assembled there. Perhaps a recognition test in which the target person appeared again as a "photographer" accompanied by camera and other props (with distractors similarly constructed), compared with one in which he appeared in a quite different role, might be more likely to produce effects of context change. Note that there is no inconsistency between this prediction and that which might be derived from Baddeley and Woodhead's (1983) distinction between "independent" and "interactive" contexts. What I have done here is to try to examine the basis of "interactive" contextual encoding.

The contextual effects I have described may therefore be interpreted as operating primarily via semantic coding. But it must be emphasised that the use of unfamiliar faces in these experiments means that we are not talking here about the "identity-specific" semantics which we normally access from familiar faces. When Davies and Milne (1982) changed to a task of episodic recognition memory for familiar faces, which appeared against the same or different background contexts, they found no effects of contextual change. For familiar faces, additional sources of semantic information are available over and above those derived directly from the visual pattern. Episodic memory for familiar faces will be mediated through identity-specific semantic codes (and/or names), and these will not be influenced by the background context against which each face is shown. Neil Kinnock is leader of the British Labour Party whether he is shown in front of a picture of a bank, a launderette, or the House of Commons. The prediction which follows from this account (cf. Bruce, Note 2; Memon &

Bruce, 1985) is that contextual effects in episodic recognition for familiar faces *might* be observed if a contextual manipulation was introduced which influenced their identity-specific semantic codes. Analogous to Tulving and Thomson's situation (Strawberry-Jam, Traffic-Jam), "ambiguous" public figures such as Ronald Reagan might be presented in one context (Hollywood movies) and recognition memory tested in another (politics). Though the difficulty of selecting materials for such an experiment would tax the ingenuity of researchers, the prediction must be that recognition accuracy or latency (more likely the latter, given possible ceiling effects on accuracy, see Bruce, 1982) would be affected by this contextual manipulation.

We can therefore accommodate effects of context in face memory experiments within a framework in which different kinds of information ("codes") are made explicit. Such a framework may provide an important potential clarification of the way in which variables such as delay, pose change, target-distractor similarity, and so forth, may affect recognition memory for faces. Different information codes may be differentially affected by the manipulation of such variables, and this might allow us to make more sense of what can be a confusing literature (e.g. see the review of effects of delay in Chapter 1). In the next part of this chapter, I move away from the topic of recognition memory, and return to consider highly familiar faces, to offer suggestions about the processes which allow us to access identity-specific semantic codes.

THEORETICAL ACCOUNTS OF THE ACCESS OF IDENTITY-SPECIFIC SEMANTIC INFORMATION

In the course of the preceding section on context effects in episodic memory, I have illustrated how five different codes, which may be established when a face is viewed, may be used in tasks of episodic recognition memory. These codes include the "pictorial" and the "structural" visual codes, the "visually derived" and "identity-specific" semantic codes, and the "name." To this list, Bruce and Young (1986) added two further codes termed "expression" and "facial speech" codes, which result respectively from the analysis of expression and the analysis of lip and tongue movements in the interpretation of speech. I will not discuss the formation of expression and facial speech codes any further here, since there is good evidence (which I reviewed in Chapter 2) that expression interpretation and lip-reading skills are activities which proceed independently from facial *recognition*.

Of the five remaining codes which are more directly relevant to facial recognition, pictorial codes probably play a role only in laboratory experiments of particular kinds, where the tasks involve episodic recognition of unfamiliar faces presented and tested in the same views. In real life we will rarely encounter identical instances of a face in this way. For the rest of this chapter, we will be concentrating on everyday acts of identifying familiar faces, rather than the laboratory task of remembering unfamiliar ones, though we will consider the relationship between these two activities again at the end of the chapter.

In the terms that we have introduced here, the task of identifying a familiar face can be seen to involve several stages:

1. Deriving structural codes.
2. Matching these to stored structural codes.
3. Accessing identity-specific semantic information.
4. Accessing a name.

I now turn to consider recent attempts by myself and my colleagues to construct theoretical accounts of this process. The accounts have borrowed heavily from the models of Morton (1969; 1979), Seymour (1979), and others which have been constructed to account for the access of semantic information from words and objects.

In 1979 I published the first of a series of articles in which I drew explicit analogies between the identification processes involved in the recognition of faces and words. I began by studying processes of visual search—subjects had to "spot" the faces of specified familiar target politicians in arrays of unfamiliar faces, and I compared the results with those obtained when targets and array items were names. I found that for both faces and names, search time increased as the number of target items which had to be searched for simultaneously was increased, and for both kinds of material, the function relating search time to target set size was negatively accelerated. I suggested that a possible explanation for these search functions was that subjects switched from an essentially visual strategy, of searching for the visual dimensions which specified a target face or name, to a semantic strategy in which they conducted the task by deciding whether or not each face (or name) was that of a politician. A visual strategy would be sensitive to the number of targets to be detected, since more visual descriptions would have to be held and checked as set size increased. If all the targets shared the same semantic description (e.g. if all were politicians), a semantic strategy would not be affected in this way, and would become increasingly efficient as the number of targets was increased.

Some support for this hypothesis was obtained for faces, by exploring the nature of the visual search process in a task of serial classification. Subjects were presented with a series of individual faces, and had to decide for each whether it was one of the target politicians. The nature of the distractor (nontarget) items was varied in terms of their visual and/or semantic similarity to the targets. Visual similarity was varied on the basis of other subjects' ratings of the faces for their visual resemblance to a series of specified targets. Semantic similarity was varied by including both politicians and nonpoliticians (actors, comedians, etc.) as distractors. When the target was a single politician, search seemed to be based primarily on visual dimensions. Visually similar distractors took longer to reject than visually dissimilar ones, but semantic similarity had an effect only if the faces were also visually similar. When subjects had to search for any one of four politician targets, a different pattern was obtained. The effect of visual similarity was still strong, but semantic similarity had an effect both for visually similar and for dissimilar items. There was no interaction between the effects of visual and semantic similarity in this situation. Similar results were obtained for words in a separate experiment (Bruce, 1981). Subjects searching for any one of four "animal" word targets were affected both by the visual similarity between distractors and targets (as defined by word length and spelling) and by their conceptual similarity—other animal words took longer to reject. These effects were again independent.

I explained this pattern of independent effects of visual and semantic similarity by proposing that access to identify-specific semantics could proceed in parallel with the visual processes of checking for specific dimensions which characterise the target set (Bruce, 1979; 1981). Both these semantic and visual processing routes independently feed information to a hypothesised decision-making system, which is seeking sufficient evidence to reject a distractor, or to accept a target. Provided that the visual checking process cannot be completed too quickly (as might be the case with a single target, for example, or where all targets were distinguished by a single attribute, such as skin colour), information about semantics will be available to influence the decision process. An important result obtained both with faces and with words was that familiarity per se had no influence on rejection latency. Distractors which were familiar celebrities were no slower to reject than unfamiliar faces (Bruce, 1979), and distractors which were words were no slower than pronounceable nonwords (Bruce, 1981). Thus the only aspect of semantics which appears to play a role in this task is that to do with the semantic category of the targets—whether the face is that of a politician or not when the targets are politicians, and whether the item is an animal name or not when the targets are animal names.

One way to account for the effects of semantic relatedness is to propose that items within the same semantic category as the targets become "primed" for recognition due to activation spreading from the lowered thresholds on the targets themselves. Such a proposal would not be controversial for the recognition of words (cf. Collins & Loftus, 1975), where we could propose that activation spreads within the semantic

R.F.—F

network to influence thresholds in word recognition units or logogens (cf. also Morton, 1969; 1979). Morton has suggested that for each known word (or perhaps morpheme) in a reader's vocabulary, there is a recognition device (visual input logogen) which contains an abstract structural (e.g. graphemic) code which distinguishes this word from all others. The recognition unit will respond when that word is seen in any typeface or handwriting, provided the appropriate structural information is encoded from the presented word. Visual input logogens (heard words are thought to be recognised via separate units) are conceived as threshold devices, whose thresholds must be overcome before recognition can occur. If a threshold was lowered, then relatively less structural information would be needed for recognition to occur. This would have the consequence of reducing tachistoscopic recognition thresholds for primed words, speeding up lexical decisions to primed words, and also, in the search situation described, slowing down rejection latencies to primed words which happen not to be targets.

In 1982, Hay and Young published the first wide-ranging theoretical framework to explain recognition of familiar faces, and made explicit the proposal that face recognition might be mediated by "face recognition units" somewhat analogous to the lexical units proposed by many people as mediating word recognition (Morton, 1969; 1979; etc.). This hypothesis provides a possible mechanism to explain the semantic similarity effects that I had observed in my experiments. Their model is shown in Fig. 12.

In the model, "representational processes" furnish visual descriptions suitable for recognition purposes, which can then be matched with similar descriptions contained within the face recognition units. As originally proposed by Hay and Young, face recognition units are units which can potentially respond when any view of a familar face is seen. They must thus contain the abstract structural codes which specify individual facial identity, just as logogens must contain graphemic (and/or phonological) codes to specify lexical identity at a level more abstract than that of a particular typeface or handwriting. There will be a separate unit for each known face, and each unit will have a threshold of excitation which must be reached before the unit will respond. Response of the unit signals that a face is familiar, and can lead to access of the appropriate semantic information specifying who the person is. Names are accessed only via semantic information about personal identity.

Thus the sequence of operations involved in correctly naming a familiar face involves:

1. Constructing a suitable representation (i.e. deriving structural codes).
2. Matching a representation within a face recognition unit.
3. Accessing the semantic (person) information.
4. Accessing and generating a name.

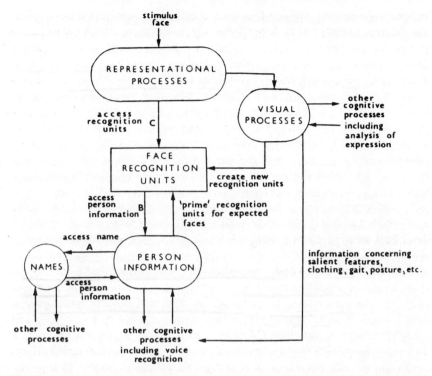

FIG. 12. Hay and Young's (1982) model of the functional components involved in face recognition. Reproduced with permission.

The evidence for this sequential processing route will be presented shortly. First we should just note that a variety of other processes are seen as operating in parallel with this sequence. The analysis of facial expression is seen as independent from that of identity, and results from other "visual processing" which is suggested to occur in parallel with that subserving the identification of a face. This parallel visual processing route is necessary to accommodate my own (Bruce, 1979) data in which independent effects of visual and semantic similarity were observed, and it also provides a possible route for the access of visually derived (as opposed to identity-specific) semantic information.

The most important aspects of the Hay and Young model were:

1. The hypothesis that familiar face recognition proceeds in parallel with the extraction of other kinds of information—a position which I have already assumed in this chapter on the basis of evidence reviewed in Chapter 2.
2. The sequence in which the access of visual, semantic, and verbal (name) codes was suggested to occur.
3. The hypothesis of face recognition units.

At the time of its publication, there was limited experimental evidence to support the model—my own data being the primary source. The model did, however, fare well in accommodating anecdotal observations of failures in everyday face recognition processes, as well as explaining the patterns of breakdown which can be observed following brain damage.

Briefly, the model suggests that the following "malfunctions" of the system could occur. First, a face could fail to access or sufficiently activate the appropriate face recognition unit, and so might fail to signal familiarity. Examples of such failures are common. We have all, occasionally, walked past friends, often where they are not expected in a particular context, and the main subjective problem experienced by "prosopagnosic" patients is that all faces appear unfamiliar to them. A second possibility is that a face recognition unit may respond sufficiently to signal familiarity, but access to semantic information about personal identity might be blocked. This state would result in our recognising the face as familiar, but being unable to remember who the person is, or why they seem familiar. Again, this seems to happen quite commonly, particularly when people we know rather slightly are met in novel contexts. Thirdly, a face recognition unit may respond, and appropriate semantic information be accessed, but the route to the name may be blocked. Here the name may be "on the tip of our tongue," a state which Yarmey (1973) found particularly easy to induce when asking people to name famous faces. As important as the states which might arise from such a model are those which cannot. If Hay and Young's framework is correct, there should be no possibility of a face being correctly named if no semantic information is available.

Shortly after the publication of this framework, Andy Young and his colleagues in Lancaster embarked upon a large scale "diary" study in which volunteers were asked to keep formal records of any errors and difficulties they experienced when recognising people in their everyday activities (Young, Hay, & Ellis, 1985). (Although their study included errors and difficulties in recognising people from sources other than the face, the majority of their records involved face perception, and I will here treat their study as if it was concerned only with the perception of faces.) In the total of 922 errors and difficulties recorded by 22 diarists over a 7-week period, there were *no* cases where a diarist reported an inability or difficulty in recalling semantic information from a face where the name of the person was available to them. Difficulties or errors permitted by Hay and Young's model were, however, all reported with reasonably high frequencies. Thus all of the diarists reported failures to recognise familiar people and/or misidentifications of one person for another. Such errors would be accounted for at the "recognition unit" stage. All the diarists reported situations in which faces seemed familiar, but no semantic or name information could be retrieved, consistent with the activation of a face recognition unit along with a failure to access appropriate person information. Finally, 19 of them recorded failures to name faces which were otherwise successfully recognised. Over 90% of the reported incidents involved errors and difficulties of these three main types.

As well as the additional data provided by this diary study, Young and his colleagues have furnished further experimental evidence consistent with a sequence of processing stages in which structural codes are constructed prior to semantic codes, which in turn precede the retrieval of names. Young, McWeeny, Hay, and Ellis (1986b) have shown that decisions which can be made at the level of the face recognition units (i.e. on the basis of structural codes) are made more quickly than are decisions which must be made at the level of semantic codes. Subjects were much quicker to decide whether or not each face they saw was familiar than whether or not each was a politician. Of more importance was their observation that a factor which speeded up semantic decisions had no effect on the speed with which familiarity decisions could be made. Familiarity decisions were made no more quickly if the familiar faces were drawn from a single semantic category than if they were drawn from mixed semantic categories, a result which seems to confirm that "familiarity only" decisions result from a level prior to that at which semantic information is revealed. In other work, Young, McWeeny, Ellis, and Hay (1986) have shown that naming faces is a considerably slower process than is semantic categorisation, even when the faces to be named and categorised are well-learned. Thus experimental evidence is consistent with the processing sequence shown in the Hay and Young model.

Hay and Young suggested that face recognition units might function in an analogous way to logogens in models of word recognition. In Nottingham, we set out to investigate whether face recognition was affected by repetition (identity priming) and associative priming in the ways which would be predicted by a logogen-type account. Thresholds in logogens may be lowered either directly, following presentation of the item itself (identity priming), or indirectly, via the semantic system, following presentation of a semantically related item (associative/semantic priming). We set out to explore whether results with faces were consistent with this conception of face recognition units.

In these experiments, we made extensive use of the "face familiarity task," which I introduced (Bruce, 1983) as a task which makes demands equivalent to those of the lexical decision task used by researchers of word recognition. In the face familiarity task, subjects are presented with a series of highly familiar faces, intermixed with equal numbers of unfamiliar faces, and their task is to decide as quickly as possible whether or not each face is familiar. Bruce and Valentine (1985) found that familiarity decisions were made more quickly to familiar faces which had earlier been presented either in the same or a different picture, compared with a control condition where no prior exposure had occurred. No facilitation was observed when earlier exposure had been to the name, rather than to the face. This result suggests that the locus of identity priming from an earlier view of the face was at a stage earlier than that to which names have access. In the Hay and Young model, the same person information is thought to be accessed by faces and by names, so clearly the repetition effect must be located elsewhere, according to this model. The face recognition units are the obvious possibility. Consistent with an effect at this level, we found that, while repetition priming effects were greatest in the "same picture" condition, the degree of priming in the "different picture" condition was unrelated to the rated similarities between the pairs of pictures used. This can be explained if we assume that, once activated, a face recognition unit's threshold is lowered, making it easier to recognise that face again later. Since a face recognition unit responds to any view of the face, it should not matter if the later presentation is in a very different or a very similar pose. (This still leaves unexplained the extra benefit of retesting in an identical view. This must be attributed to a visual memory component, and, as we will see later, the contribution of this component may have been underestimated by Bruce and Valentine.) A. Ellis, Young, Flude, and Hay (1987) went on to see whether priming in these experiments was specifically between one face and another, or whether prior exposure to a picture of a person's *body* (clothed!) would prime later recognition of their face. They found no effects of body-priming on face recognition, lending further support to an interpretation in terms of "face," rather than "person" recognition units.

Similar support for the hypothesis of face recognition units was initially derived from experiments on associative priming. In a preliminary experiment (Bruce, 1983), I found that familiarity decisions were made more quickly to faces preceded by close associates than to faces preceded by unrelated familiar faces. For example, subjects were quicker to decide that Princess Diana's face was familiar if it was preceded in the test series by Prince Charles' than if preceded by Stanley Laurel's face. In subsequent work (Bruce & Valentine, 1986) we examined in more detail the nature of associative priming between faces. By presenting faces in pairs, with a response required only to the second face of each pair, we were able to vary the time interval (stimulus onset asynchrony—SOA) between the onset of the "prime" (first) and "target" (second) faces, and compare the effects of a related prime with those of both unrelated (familiar) and neutral (unfamiliar) primes. We found that even where SOA was reduced to 250msec., which is far too short for subjects to name the prime face or strategically to predict which face might appear next, there was significant facilitation from a related prime. At no SOA was there any evidence of inhibition—the "related" and "neutral" prime conditions produced similar response latencies. My postgraduate student Tim Brennen has recently replicated the pattern of effects at 250msec. SOA, and has also demonstrated that the particular choice of neutral condition used by myself and Tim Valentine is unlikely to have been responsible for this pattern (cf. Jonides & Mack, 1984).

The observation of significant facilitation effects at short SOAs is consistent with an "automatic" effect of spreading activation within the semantic system (cf. de Groot, 1984; Neely, 1976; Posner & Snyder, 1975). According to the Hay and Young model, we might propose that recognition of the prime face (say, Prince Charles) activates the person information appropriate to this face, and activation then spreads to associated person information, which will include that to do with Princess Diana. Activation of person information will then lead to reduced thresholds in the appropriate face recognition units. Bruce and Valentine (1986) found that semantic priming effects were greater when stimulus quality was reduced by blurring the target faces. This interaction between stimulus quality and associative priming is consistent with (though not exclusive to) an effect located at a stage which would be affected by stimulus degradation—the face recognition units.

Early results were, then, consistent with Hay and Young's hypothesis of face recognition units which functioned as threshold devices. However, more recent work has revealed some problems with this position. The main problem comes with the interpretation of the effects of identity priming. As described in more detail in Chapter 5, although Bruce and Valentine (1985) found no correlation between visual similarity of views and the amount of facilitation obtained from one to another, their procedure was undoubtedly insensitive. A. Ellis et al. (1987) have since used a better experimental design and found that similar views gave more priming than dissimilar views, a result which is more consistent with a visual memory than a recognition unit interpretation.

Bruce (1986b) showed that identity and semantic priming effects did not dissipate in the same way as the delay between prime and target was increased. Identity priming effects showed no sign of decay over the range of 0 to 11 slides which intervened between prime and target items (corresponding to lags of from 5–60sec.). Semantic priming effects were observed only at the shortest lag, where the prime item immediately preceded the target. This result exactly mirrors that found by Dannenbring and Briand (1982) using words in a lexical decision task. While this result makes much ecological sense (Morton, personal communication), since persistent semantic priming would make a nonsense in terms of the needs of a reader or a face perceiver, it requires that additional assumptions be made about the functioning of face recognition units. Threshold changes produced by direct prior activation of the unit itself must be distinguished from threshold changes produced indirectly via the semantic system. Alternatively, given A. Ellis et al.'s results with identity priming, we might argue that identity priming is not a recognition unit effect at all, but is an episodic memory effect. While Forster and Davis (1984) review some ways of teasing apart the lexical and memorial components of repetition priming using words, we are as yet some way off similar experimental sophistication using faces. In the next chapter, we will consider how an alternative "instance-based" account of face recognition might be better able to accommodate these results.

A second problem for face recognition units stems from a further set of diary records obtained by Young et al. (1985). They found that a common experience when viewing faces is to notice that a face bears a marked *resemblance* to another, known face. Sometimes these resemblances are so strong that a person is seen as another's "double," yet there is no false recognition of the double *as* the person they resemble. It is difficult to accommodate such experiences within a framework in which recognition units function as simple triggers, since the resemblance experiences show that a recognition unit can access appropriate semantic and name information and yet not signal "recognition" at all.

To accommodate their "resemblance only" records, Young et al. (1985) modified the concept of recognition units away from the threshold devices proposed by Hay and Young. They proposed instead that recognition units send out a graded signal according to the degree to which the structural codes derived from an encountered face match those housed within each unit. Effectively, they argued that the recognition units signal the extent to which a seen face *resembles* the stored description. Such graded signals will then be interpreted in the light of other information, including that from contextual sources. A "double" of Margaret Thatcher would not be recognised *as* Margaret Thatcher in your local shopping precinct—unless you happen to live in Finchley (her parliamentary constituency) and it was a week before a general election. Thus Young et al. are suggesting that context effects may operate at a level apart from the recognition units, and perhaps in a manner more analogous to conscious problem-solving than that suggested by the semantic priming data of Bruce and Valentine (1986). One possible reconciliation here would be to propose two quite distinct ways in which context might facilitate recognition. The first, analogous to what Forster (1981) calls "lexical" priming, might be an automatic effect obtained only with closely associated faces, affecting activation levels within the face recognition units. The second, perhaps analogous to a "thematic" level in sentence processing, might produce the more obviously conscious and strategic use of context to supplement information obtained via the face recognition units, but would be seen as a post-access effect. Such an hypothesis would not be inconsistent with proposals elsewhere in the priming literature, where it has been common to distinguish at least two different kinds of contextual influence; a fast, automatic effect and a slower, strategic, expectancy effect (e.g. Posner & Snyder, 1975).

Andy Young and myself (Bruce & Young, 1986) have recently produced a synthesis and extension of the earlier models of Hay and Young (1982) and Young et al. (1985). It also shares much in common with recent accounts by Ellis (1986a) and Rhodes (1985). Our model is shown in Fig. 13. In the model, *structural encoding* processes are held to furnish visual descriptions at different levels of abstraction. Viewer-centred descriptions are used for the analysis of expression and facial speech (see Chapter 2), but from these, expression-independent descriptions are derived which can access descriptions in similar format housed within the *face recognition units*.

The face recognition units send out graded signals of resemblance to decision processes set up within the cognitive system (cf. Young et al., 1985), but their basic level of activation may also be affected (primed) by recent use or by contextual information feeding back from the *person identity nodes*. The person identity nodes are the level at which *person* recognition, as opposed to face recognition, can occur, and they may be accessed by information obtained from a name, a voice, clothing, and so forth, as well as from the face (only access via the face is shown in the model). When a person identity node is accessed, the identity-specific semantic codes become available. *Names* can only be generated via the person identity nodes.

Following Morton (1969; 1979), we used the term *cognitive system* as a convenient label for a collection of cognitive functions not otherwise specified in the model. Like Baddeley and Hitch's "central executive" in the "working memory" model (Baddeley & Hitch, 1974), it is currently a catch-all component. Several distinct functions may be seen as served by the cognitive system: it houses semantic memory, selects between different information sources, takes decisions, and initiates responses. Since the person identity nodes form part of a more general semantic memory system, they could really be seen as lying within the cognitive system. However, because of the distinct role played by the person identity nodes in facial recognition, they have been drawn as a separate component. Another outcrop of the cognitive system is the final component drawn in Fig. 13, that labelled *directed visual processing*. In order to compare and remember faces, we may attend selectively to certain aspects of their structure—if sent to the station to meet someone, we may look out for people with the right hairstyle, or if acting as a subject in a face memory experiment, we may carefully look for such things as moles or blemishes

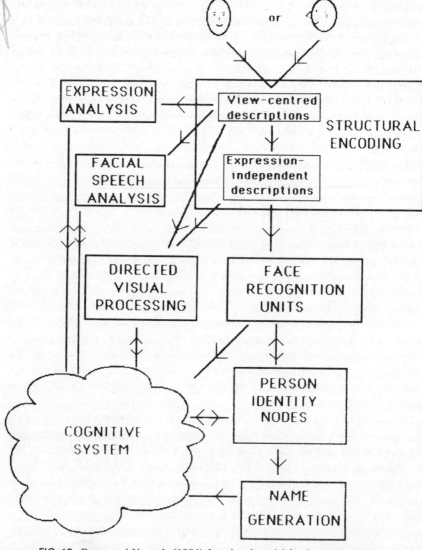

FIG. 13. Bruce and Young's (1986) functional model for face recognition.

that we may be able to remember later. This attentional component has also been taken "outside" the cognitive system, in order to highlight a route which may be important in episodic memory for unfamiliar faces, and which prosopagnosic patients may try to use to overcome their problems in recognising faces.

This model is able to accommodate all the evidence I have discussed here and in Chapter 2, as well as other neuropsychological evidence (see

Bruce & Young, 1986, for details). We see this model as an hypothesis about the sequential access and construction of the different codes which are important for different uses made of facial information. Thus expression codes and facial speech codes are generated by the corresponding components in the model, essentially independently from codes which underly the recognition of individual identity of a face. To access identity, structural codes must be derived from the image, and matched to those housed in the recognition units. Identity-specific semantic codes may then be accessed from the person identity nodes, and finally, name codes may be generated.

How does this model account for the derivation of those codes which were suggested as important to remember unfamiliar faces—pictorial and visually-derived semantic codes? Andy Young and myself (Bruce & Young, 1986) suggested that pictorial codes are a by-product of the structural encoding process—they are episodic records of the particular photographs which have been seen. Visually derived semantic codes include the perceived age and sex of a face, which might perhaps likewise form part of some early categorisation process (see Ellis, 1986a), which I consider later in this chapter. In contrast, the specification of the apparent honesty or intelligence of a face must involve the cognitive system.

This functional model provides a good account of existing evidence from diverse sources, and thereby provides a clear framework for understanding the recognition of familiar faces. This framework, which has emerged in part from analogies with word processing, can itself be used to clarify the similarities and differences between the recognition of faces, other objects, and words. For example, the model shows names to be retrieved only via the person identity nodes: There is no direct route from faces to names. In this respect the processes of face recognition resemble those of object recognition but differ from visual word recognition, where names can be generated directly from the surface form as well as via semantics (see Bruce & Young, 1986, for details of the evidence). These different routes involved in the naming of faces, objects, and names are given further support by patterns of interference in naming and categorisation tasks reported by Young, Hay, and Ellis (1986). In brief, written names interfere with the naming, but not the semantic categorisation, of faces, and photographs of faces interfere with the semantic categorisation, but not the naming, of names. These results mirror those found in tasks of naming and categorising objects and their labels.

A model of this kind is of considerable heuristic value in clarifying what it is we understand about face recognition, and, perhaps more importantly, what problems need to be addressed in future research. One set of issues clearly involves the further specification of the components of this model. Other issues may require a more fundamental revision of the framework itself. For example, the model fares least well at accounting for the creation of pictorial and visually derived semantic codes hypothesised as playing a major role in episodic memory for unfamiliar faces. This is perhaps to be expected, since the model was aimed at explaining the recognition of familiar faces, not recognition memory. However, one future direction is clearly given by the need to try to integrate our accounts of recognition memory for unfamiliar faces, and identification of familiar ones. In the next section, I will consider in detail some problems raised by the Bruce and Young model, and some of our recent experimental attempts to clarify these issues. This next section itself illustrates the usefulness of an explicit framework of this kind in guiding our research. Then, in Chapters 5 and 6, I will introduce some quite different perspectives which may prove useful in the future development of these theoretical ideas.

PROBLEMS FOR THE BRUCE AND YOUNG MODEL

Context Effects: How Can We Reconcile the Episodic with the Semantic?

Early on in this chapter, I described research which showed how altering the pictured background context against which a previously unfamiliar face was portrayed could reduce the accuracy of subsequent recognition memory performance, particularly if subjects had been encouraged to rate apparent personality attributes of the faces at presentation. I appealed to the formation and matching of "visually derived semantic codes" as an explanation of such effects. Later in the chapter, I reviewed effects of contextual manipulations on the recognition of highly familiar faces—a face such as that of Princess Diana is more readily recognised as familiar if the preceding face is that of Prince Charles. In this case, the explanation is couched in terms of possible priming of face recognition units, mediated via activity in the "person identity nodes," which house information in the form of "identity-specific semantic codes."

Although these two kinds of contextual effect appear to be accounted for quite well by appeal to these different semantic routes, it is not difficult to think of hypothetical situations in which such distinctions become blurred. The problem arises because for less familiar, and less "public" faces than those used in semantic priming experiments, identity is often bound up with the places where the people are normally encountered, and even the role we ourselves play when we encounter them. Examples of this were frequent in Young et al.'s (1985) diary study, but an example from my own experience will suffice. While walking in my local town, I passed a man I knew well enough to greet. The recognition was mutual, and we exchanged a few words, but I was unable to remember who he was. I was, however, convinced that he was someone associated with a local shop, and, even more definitely, sure that I normally saw him when I was with my dog. I systematically recalled each of the shops near to my house, that I might visit when with the dog, but failed to associate him with any of them. It was only later that night that I remembered the pet shop, some distance further from my home, and immediately realised that the man was the pet shop owner. I would have had no difficulty recognising the man in context—and in a sense, his identity to me is equivalent to the context in which I encounter him.

The distinction between "episodic" and "semantic" knowledge becomes blurred in a case such as this, and forces us to consider carefully whether the distinction between episodic memory for faces, and semantic processes of identifying familiar faces, is one which is really justified. In the next chapter, we will consider the potential utility of memory models which see all the apparent phenomena of a distinct semantic memory as emerging from the retention of all previous instances or "episodes."

How are Visually Derived Semantic Codes Derived?

The Bruce and Young framework emphasises that there is a distinction to be drawn between visually derived and identity-specific semantic codes. The former include all aspects of the meaning of that face which are specified by the actual configuration of the face, as contrasted with those aspects which are a consequence of the individual history of the face's owner. Visually derived semantic codes thus potentially include the information that this configuration is a face (as opposed to some other object), the apparent sex of the face, the apparent age of the face, its apparent honesty or attractiveness, and the fact that it resembles certain other known faces. Since such classifications are common in our everyday activities, it would be useful if our model had something to say about them.

As noted, it is unlikely that a single route underlies the recovery of these very different sorts of visually derived semantic codes, and Bruce and Young (1986) specifically suggested that judgements about the facial configuration per se, and its age and sex, might form part of the initial "structural encoding" component, possibly in the manner suggested by Ellis (1986a; 1986b).

Ellis's model is in many respects equivalent to that of Bruce and Young, except for its explicit proposal that there is some kind of sequential relationship between judgements about overall facial configuration, sex, age and race, and identity (see Fig. 14). Recently, in collaboration with Andy Young and Hadyn Ellis, I have tested the validity of this proposed hierarchy.

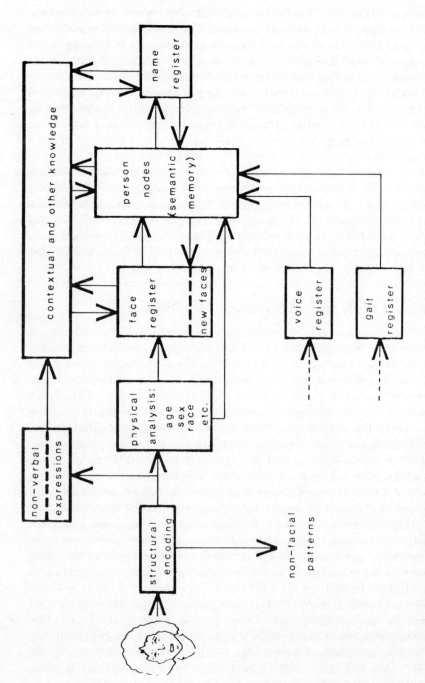

FIG. 14. Ellis's (1986a) model of the functional components involved in face recognition. Reproduced with permission.

In one set of experiments (Bruce, 1986a), I set out to explore whether familiarity with faces had any effect on the ease with which faces could be categorised *as faces* (as opposed to jumbled faces), as *male* faces, or as *smiling* faces. In each of three experiments (face classification, sex classification, and expression classification), a group of faces highly familiar to students in my home department were compared with a group unfamiliar to these students. The experiments were repeated in Lancaster, where both groups of faces were unfamiliar, to provide a baseline against which to assess the effects in Nottingham.

Consistent with our hypothesis that expression analysis proceeds independently from facial identification, familiarity with the faces had no effect on the speed with which expression judgements could be made. There was evidence, however, that familiarity with the faces could facilitate sex judgements, although the effects were only significant over subjects and not over materials. However, an effect of familiarity which was significant on both a subjects and an items analysis was observed in the face classification task. Subjects were faster at deciding that familiar faces were faces, and slower to decide that they were jumbled faces, relative to the baseline performance observed in Lancaster.

Such effects of familiarity (which must result from the last stage in the hierarchy) on tasks which should be performed at a logically earlier stage cannot readily be explained by a strict perceptual hierarchy. One possibility is to modify the hierarchy into some kind of "cascade" system (cf. McClelland & Rumelhart, 1981). In a cascade system such as that of the "interactive activation" model of word recognition, which I describe in more detail in Chapter 5, earlier processes need not be completed before later ones begin, and information is fed back as well as forward between the different hierarchical levels. Alternatively, we might consider the recognition of the face as "a face" to proceed in parallel with recognition of its identity, with information from these different parallel routes being compared by an explicit decision-making system (cf. Bruce, 1979). The "jumbled" faces used in the experiment are still quite recognisable since they preserve the features, and some of the configuration, of the face. Thus the influence of familiarity could be explained by positive information from the "identity" route facilitating the decision that familiar faces *are* faces, but making it more difficult to decide that they are not.

In further experimental work (Bruce, Ellis, Gibling, & Young, in press) we have explored further consequences of a proposed hierarchical relationship between judgements of apparent sex, and those of identity. The hypothesis of a perceptual hierarchy implies that faces which are difficult (i.e. slow) to categorise in terms of sex, should also be slow to categorise as familiar. This didn't seem to mesh with our intuitions, and indeed an initial thought experiment almost suffices: Boy George does not seem difficult to recognise.

We set about checking these intuitions formally. We first asked a number of students to rate the apparent masculinity or femininity of a large number of familiar and unfamiliar faces drawn from media sources. All faces were trimmed around the edge so that resulting hairstyles were fairly neutral in terms of sex, and none of the male faces wore a beard or moustache. The familiarity of each face was also rated. From the resulting ratings, we were able to select matched sets of high-masculine and low-masculine familiar male faces, and high-masculine and low-masculine unfamiliar male faces. These 40 male faces (10 in each set) were then intermixed with 40 female faces which acted as "fillers."

The 80 faces were then shown to 2 groups of subjects. The first group was instructed to classify each face by sex, as quickly as possible, and the second group was asked to classify each face as familiar, as quickly as possible. As expected, while we found that the high-masculine faces could be judged as male very much more quickly than the low-masculine faces, there was no difference between these two groups in the times taken to categorise them as familiar or unfamiliar.

In a further experiment, four groups of subjects were compared. The first two groups were asked to judge sex or familiarity, and thus replicated the conditions of the initial experiment. A third group was asked to respond positively if each face was "male *or* familiar," and a fourth group was asked to respond positively if each face was "male *and* familiar." In each group of subjects, we were particularly interested in the effects of high- and low-masculinity on the familiar male faces, since these should always elicit positive responses.

The results were best explained by proposing that sex judgements and familiarity judgements result from *parallel* procedures, with sex judgements normally being completed more quickly than familiarity judgements. The high-low masculinity dimension had a significant effect only on those tasks where a response could be made on the basis of a sex judgement alone (i.e. is the face male? is the face male or familiar?), and had no significant effect where the response must await the outcome of a familiarity decision (i.e. is the face familiar? is the face male and familiar?).

These recent experiments have thus lent no support to Ellis's proposal that sex judgements precede familiarity judgements in any kind of strict perceptual hierarchy. Parallel procedures provide a better account of the data, though a cascade account could also be offered. Indeed, Ellis (1986a) seems to suggest this possibility in his (Fig. 14) model, by including the arrow linking the "physical analysis" stage directly with the "person nodes," implying that physical analysis might continue in parallel with the access of identity. Ellis included this route to accommodate my results (Bruce, 1979) showing apparently parallel physical and semantic analyses of faces in a search task. Under some circumstances, he suggested, semantic information might be accessed before physical analysis was complete. Our recent research demonstrates that such a route must play a rather more fundamental role than Ellis had anticipated. It appears that Bruce and Young (1986) were probably right to remain vague about the relationship between judgements of sex and age and those of identity.

The results of this research are rather negative. These experiments do not tell us much about how it is that we reach decisions about the age, sex, or race of a face, merely that a strict "hierarchy" appears to be wrong. If we turn to the literature on perceptual processing of faces, reviewed in Chapter 3, we will find little there either to tell us what are the important dimensions for classifying a face in terms of sex or age—most work which has been done on perception of faces has focused on those features used to identify individual faces, rather than to identify categories of face. In Chapter 6, I will describe how work of a more "ecological" nature has been revealing about the basis of our perception of the age of a face, and suggest how work in a similar vein may prove fruitful in explaining how we perceive the sex of a face.

What of the other kinds of semantic information that may be "visually derived" from faces? As we discussed earlier, perceived resemblances between unfamiliar and known faces can be accommodated within the Bruce and Young framework, since it is the business of face recognition units to signal resemblance. And certain kinds of visually derived semantic information could be seen as resulting from the components which analyse facial expression and facial speech. But the framework provides no route whatsoever for a face to be judged as "honest" or looking "like a policeman." All we can say is that such judgements are made in the cognitive system. Again it appears that we must look beyond this framework for an account of how we make these kinds of attributions to unfamiliar faces.

How are Structural Codes Derived?

We have seen earlier that the Bruce and Young framework experiences some difficulties in accommodating all our everyday understanding of faces. It is most successful as a model of the recognition of familiar faces. What, then, have we to say about the nature of the visual codes which are abstracted from faces, and which allow familiar faces to be recognised in such a variety of views?

Theoretical frameworks of the "logogen" type have deliberately side-stepped the tricky issue of the nature of the representations upon which recognition can be based, and concentrated instead on the relationships between sensory and semantic coding processes of various types. In Hay and Young's original framework for face recognition, little was said about the nature of the codes which were housed within the face recognition units, whose access mediated face recognition. We discussed earlier how Ellis (1986a; 1986b) has suggested a kind of perceptual hierarchy, in which progressively finer details extracted from a face allow it to be classified as a face, as a face of apparent sex, race, and age, and finally as a particular individual's face. This hierarchy of representational stages could map onto the different categorisations which can be supported by progressively higher bands of spatial frequencies, as discussed by Sergent (1986; see Chapter 3). However, as noted above, experimental evidence does not support a simple hierarchy of the type proposed by Ellis, and Sergent's description of spatial frequency channels could be consistent with sequential, cascading, or parallel processes with differing time-courses.

Bruce and Young (1986) made tentative proposals about the nature and derivation of the structural codes contained within face recognition units. In so doing, we drew on the framework for object recognition proposed by Marr and Nishihara (1978). Marr and Nishihara argued that the representations underlying the recognition of natural objects should be modular in nature, with interconnected descriptions at separate levels describing overall shapes and details of component parts. In similar vein, Bruce and Young suggested that the structural code specifying, say, Margaret Thatcher's face was not a unitary code, but might comprise a representation of overall configuration and representations of particular distinctive features. As I noted in Chapter 3, there is good evidence for the extraction of both these kinds of properties from faces.

Marr and Nishihara (1978) also proposed that representations which subserve object recognition should be object-centred, rather than viewer-centred. Viewer-centred representations will change with viewpoint, and thus require that descriptions be stored of the object from a large number of viewpoints. An object-centred representation, on the other hand, will remain invariant with respect to viewpoint, and thus only a single representation will need to be stored for each known object. Despite the parsimony of an object-centred representational scheme for object recognition, Bruce and Young (1986) argued that the specific (axis-based) representational scheme proposed by Marr and Nishihara (which I will describe in greater detail in Chapter 6) is not suitable to cope with the fine discriminations needed for face recognition, where all the items to be discriminated have similar overall shapes. We also noted that faces only need to be recognised over a small range of viewpoints (and indeed face recognition is particularly impaired following inversion, as I noted in Chapter 1). While Bruce and Young rejected the notion that face recognition was based on "raw" view-specific information, and, in particular proposed that representations for recognition were independent of the *expression* portrayed, we did suggest that representations for recognition might be based on two or more discrete head angles. One influence on our thinking came from the results of Perrett's group in St. Andrews (Perrett et al., 1984; 1985). They have found cells in the infero-temporal cortex of monkeys' brains which are sensitive to the faces of specific individual human keepers. Many of these cells are tuned to a particular view of a particular person, with some sensitive only to profile views, others to full-face, and so forth. Bruce and Young therefore proposed that a familiar face might be represented via an interconnected set of expression-independent structural codes, with separate representations of discrete head angles (including the profile and full-face views) and both "global" and detailed "local" information represented for each angle.

While Bruce and Young's suggestion about the nature of structural codes was fairly specific, it was based on limited evidence (some of which, on the importance of both featural and configural information, I have already reviewed in Chapter 3). Is there any human experimental evidence that distinct head angles form the basis for representations for recognition?

In a recent set of experiments, Tim Valentine, Alan Baddeley and myself (Bruce, Valentine, & Baddeley, 1987) report results which are *not* easily compatible with a proposal that full-face and profile views of familiar faces are separately represented. The work was aimed at clarifying the basis of the $\frac{3}{4}$ view advantage which has occasionally been observed in recognition memory for unfamiliar faces (Krouse, 1981; Logie, Baddeley, & Woodhead, 1987; see also Fagan, 1979, for an analogous effect with infants). A general $\frac{3}{4}$ view advantage could make some theoretical sense. Paradoxically, a system which separately represented full-face and profile views could show an advantage for $\frac{3}{4}$ views if these were within range of both these sets of specialist detectors. Alternatively, perhaps the $\frac{3}{4}$-view effect suggests that the notion of full-face and profile detectors is inappropriate. Maybe it is the $\frac{3}{4}$ view which plays a "canonical" role in face recognition (cf. Palmer, Rosch, & Chase, 1981). However, such speculations are not really appropriate unless we have established that $\frac{3}{4}$ views play a privileged role in the recognition of familiar, as well as unfamiliar, faces.

A preliminary experiment with this aim required that subjects make speeded familiarity judgements to a series of familiar (academic staff) and unfamiliar faces, presented either in full-face or $\frac{3}{4}$ views. Palmer et al. (1981) found that canonical views of objects led to faster object naming, and so we expected to find $\frac{3}{4}$ views leading to faster familiarity decisions. In fact no differences were observed between the full-face and $\frac{3}{4}$ views for either the familiar or the unfamiliar faces. A second experiment was conducted, in which subjects were asked to decide whether or not two consecutively presented faces were of the same person (expressions always differed between the two views). When the faces were unfamiliar to the subjects tested, a $\frac{3}{4}$ view advantage was observed on positive trials—two $\frac{3}{4}$

views were matched more quickly than two full-face views, and two profile views were slowest of all. The advantage of $\frac{3}{4}$ views was not observed on negative ("different") trials, nor was it found on positive or negative trials when the faces were familiar to the subjects. In all these conditions, two full-face views and two $\frac{3}{4}$ views produced equivalent performance, with profiles again slow.

These experiments have thus produced no evidence that $\frac{3}{4}$ views play a privileged role in the recognition of familiar faces, despite the observation that artists tend to use $\frac{3}{4}$ view more than other views in their work (Baddeley & Woodhead, 1983; Perkins, 1975). The $\frac{3}{4}$ view advantage which has been observed for unfamiliar face recognition seems attributable to task demands—$\frac{3}{4}$ views depict more features which may be used for matching pictured faces than do full-face or profile views. However, full-face and $\frac{3}{4}$ views seem to be equally good representations for recognition of familiar faces, with profiles considerably poorer. While this observation suggests that $\frac{3}{4}$ views do not serve as "canonical" representations for recognition, it is also bad for the proposal that full-face and profile views are separately represented. While the poor performance with profiles could be attributed to the relative frequencies of full-face and profile detectors, the equivalent performance on $\frac{3}{4}$ views and full-face views is not really compatible with the kind of generalisation function one might expect from full-face detectors.

Thus Bruce and Young's tentative proposals about the nature of the structural codes used to effect face recognition are not supported by any very convincing human experimental evidence. And, whatever the nature of these codes, we have offered no suggestions about how they might be *derived* from images of faces. This is a weakness shared by many other models which emphasise cognitive processes, and indeed was evident in much of the work on perceptual processing of faces I described in Chapter 3. I will try to rectify this weakness in Chapter 6.

Where Does a Face Recognition Unit Come From?

A final, and perhaps more fundamental problem, is that we have not addressed how a face becomes familiar. In the Bruce and Young framework it has been assumed that familiar faces are recognised via face recognition units, and unfamiliar faces presented once in recognition memory experiments are recognised via a combination of information in pictorial, structural, and visually derived semantic codes. But at what stage does a face become familiar enough to have a recognition unit devoted to it? Ellis (1986a; personal communication), in contrast, assumes that even a single exposure to a face leads to its representation within the "face register," which is a component of his model analogous to the face recognition units. But this proposal does not allow us to explain the dissociations (both clinical and experimental) between unfamiliar and familiar face processing discussed in this chapter, and in earlier ones.

In the next chapter, I consider how a theory of the *microstructure* (Rumelhart & McClelland, 1985) of devices which appear to operate like recognition units might allow us to account more satisfactorily for the emergence of qualitatively different processing of familiar and unfamiliar faces.

In summary, then, while the Bruce and Young framework is perhaps the most complete theory of face perception and recognition to date, and has proved enormously valuable in helping us interpret existing evidence and make new predictions, it is clearly deficient in some respects. While purporting to accommodate episodic as well as semantic memory phenomena within the framework provided by the different "codes," Bruce and Young's model is markedly more successful at accounting for identification of familiar faces than recognition memory for unfamiliar ones. In Chapter 5, I will consider how an instance-based model of recognition might better be able to accommodate episodic as well as semantic phenomena within a unified framework. In Chapter 6, I go on to suggest how a computational approach to face recognition may allow us to specify the nature of the structural codes derived from faces, and how they are derived.

5 Remembering Instances

In the last chapter I described recent attempts by psychologists at Aberdeen, Lancaster, and Nottingham universities to develop a functional model outlining the components involved in identifying familiar faces. The kind of model developed there typifies what McClelland and Rumelhart (1985) have labelled the "abstractive" approach which has been common to many accounts of word and object recognition. The idea is that some kind of abstract recognition unit contains the "essence" of a face, or other item, which allows the recognition of any instance of that item.

Recognition units discard the individuating characteristics of a particular instance, and so retention of these must be accounted for by appeal to other routes. For example, to explain why identical pictures of a person produced greater repetition priming than different pictures, we may appeal to benefits accruing from the "pictorial codes" also stored whenever a picture of a face is seen.

Just as the recognition units are held to contain abstract "structural" codes specifying each known face, so the "person identity nodes" are seen as containing the essential semantic information specifying individual identity. Thus the person identity node for Neil Kinnock accesses the information that he is a politician, currently leader of the British Labour Party, is Welsh, and so forth, and will connect to nodes for his wife Glenys and his deputy Roy Hattersley. All these "facts" about Kinnock, his wife, or his colleagues are held to have been abstracted from past episodes in which the facts were assimilated, and are seen as in some way distinct from the memories which may be formed of particular episodes involving Kinnock. Thus a vivid visual recollection of Kinnock's ignominious dunking on the beach during a Labour Party Conference would be seen as stemming from a separate "episodic" memory component (cf. Tulving, 1972). We have already noted the problem of accounting in a satisfactory way for a broad range of context effects within a model in which there is such a clear division between episodic and semantic information.

Abstractive accounts are not the only kind of theory of visual word or object recognition. A direct alternative would be to claim that all instances of an object or word concept are stored, and that recognition is achieved by some conspiracy of the individual memory traces. Such accounts have a potential advantage over more traditional conceptions of perception and memory, since they allow the possibility of accounting for "episodic" and "semantic" phenomena within a single conceptual framework (Jacoby, 1983a; 1983b). In this chapter I will describe some recent "instance-based" accounts of phenomena in the general literature on memory and recognition which are more traditionally considered within an abstractive framework, and consider both the advantages and the drawbacks of developing such an account of facial recognition.

HEADED RECORDS

While Morton (1969; 1979), with his logogen model, has been one of the primary exponents of an abstractive model of word perception, he has recently advocated a less structured, more episodic account of semantic memory. Morton, Hammersley, and Bekerian (1985) began by trying to apply theories of associative semantic networks to the pervasive everyday experience of failing to remember people's names. They claim that the phenomenon of being unable to remember a person's name, while being able to recall many other details about them, poses insurmountable problems for current conceptions of semantic memory. Once the right "node" to do with the person has been reached, all associated information including their name should become available.

In Hay and Young's (1982) and Bruce and Young's (1986) models of face recognition, names are housed within a different component from other information about personal identity, thus allowing their recall to be impaired selectively. Rather than adopt such a solution, Morton et al. used such common problems of name retrieval to inspire a radically different conception of semantic memory. They suggest that information about people, events, and so forth is stored in independent records, which are not associated with one another in any way. Each record has a heading, which allows access of the information stored within the record. Headings are in a code different from their associated records, and cannot themselves be retrieved (perhaps because of the nature of this access code). To explain why names may be particularly difficult to remember, Morton et al. suggest that names may normally be incorporated within the headings to records of personal information. Since headings cannot be retrieved, but can only be used to access records, one must suppose that correct name recall will only occur following access to a record in which the name is also represented as part of the record itself. Names may be included with the personal information in some, but not all, records about the person, and the personal information might contain the names of other people who are associated or related to the individual in some way.

The proposal that names are hard to remember because normally they form headings of records seems even more arbitrary than our (Bruce and Young) assumption that names are hard to remember because they are housed within a separate component, so the framework outlined here is not, on these grounds, of any more immediate appeal than that described in the last chapter. Morton et al.'s framework is also rather unsatisfactory since, while doing away with an "abstractive" semantic memory system, it assumes that initial identification of words or objects (i.e. the perceptual interface) occurs via abstractive devices such as logogens.

The literature contains many other examples of mixed abstractive and instance-based systems. McClelland and Rumelhart's (1981) model of word recognition appealed to an instance-based account of certain linguistic rule-based phenomena, while retaining essentially abstractive word detector units (cf. logogens) as an essential part of the model. However, McClelland and Rumelhart's more recent work (1985; 1986; Rumelhart & McClelland, 1986) has taken the more radical step of dispensing with abstractive units entirely, and attempting to account for logogen-like properties in terms of the superposition of discrete instances. Before considering their theory, I will discuss some of the empirical evidence for an instance-based position.

EVIDENCE FOR INSTANCES

An important feature of abstractive word-detector or object recognition units such as logogens and pictogens is that, within fairly broad limits, they should not be sensitive to physical similarities between successive instances of the word or object to which they respond. Thus repetition priming for words is affected little by variation in typeface between presentation of the prime and target instance (e.g. Clarke & Morton, 1983; Scarborough, Cortese, & Scarborough, 1977), and dissimilar instances of the same object class show as much mutual priming as do similar instances (Warren & Morton, 1982). Visual similarity effects, where found, are a property of *episodic memory*, not recognition units. Warren and Morton's finding of extra facilitation from identical compared with similar pictures must be attributed to some form of visual memory. The abstractive, recognition unit hypothesis is thus strengthened by demonstrations of effects which are not those expected of an episodic memory system, and weakened to the extent that effects are explicable in terms of general memory mechanisms.

Jacoby (1983a; 1983b) has questioned the recognition unit metaphor, by demonstrating how repetition priming effects can be shown to be entirely consistent with an episodic memory account. Thus, like recognition memory, repetition priming of words is affected by the proportion of previously presented words in the test list, by the retention interval, and by the number of lists interpolated between first and second presentation; and neither recognition memory nor repetition priming is affected by changes in the background context at test (Jacoby, 1983a). (Note that Jacoby's failure to find an effect of contextual change on recognition memory for words is consistent with other findings mentioned in Chapter 4. Generally, contextual change has an effect on verbal recognition memory only if the context at test induces a different semantic interpretation of the word from that induced by the study context.) Still more convincing is Jacoby's (1983b) demonstration that effects of encoding activity can be observed in repetition priming which are not predicted by a logogen-like account. Jacoby presented members of antonym pairs in one of three conditions: with no associated context (e.g. the word COLD alone), with their antonym partner as context (the pair HOT COLD), or following their generation from the antonym context (the word HOT presented, and the subject required to generate COLD). According to Morton's account, the first two conditions should lead to equal facilitation of later tachistosopic recognition of the word "cold," since in both cases, the visual input logogen for the word COLD will earlier have been activated to the same extent. The third condition might lead to less priming, since the subject has generated rather than visually perceived the word COLD, and so the input logogen will not have been activated. In contrast, an account of repetition effects based on overlap between presentation and test encoding activities (cf. Kolers, 1976) would predict greater priming in the first condition and least in the third. In a series of experiments, Jacoby found that presentation of the word alone led to most facilitation, and generation of the word to least, with words presented in context producing intermediate effects.

In this case, the pattern of repetition priming effects actually contrasts with performance in a task of recognition memory, where there is better retention of words which the subject has actively generated than those which have simply been read. Thus, in criticising models of the logogen type, Jacoby does retain within his own framework both a conceptual and an empirical distinction between perceptual and memorial *processes*. However, rather than attribute the differences between perceptual recognition and episodic retrieval to different stores, he attributes these differences to different aspects of stored information which may prove useful in different situations. Perceptual recognition is primarily a "data-driven" task, and will be sensitive to differences between the data to be encoded from one occasion to the next. Episodic recognition memory, or recall, is primarily "conceptually driven," and will be sensitive to the degree to which processing at encoding recruits the retrieval processes which may be needed at test.

According to models of the logogen kind, the recognition threshold of a particular logogen is lowered each time the word (or, more strictly, morpheme) is recognised. It is this lowering of the threshold which accounts for effects of repetition priming. In addition, however, when a threshold is lowered following exposure to a word, it gradually returns to a level slightly below its starting point. Thus words which are frequently encountered end up with lower recognition thresholds than those which are infrequently encountered. However, Jacoby (1983a) criticises logogen-type interpretations of standard repetition priming effects on the grounds that such effects are too large in size, and too long lasting, to account plausibly for the gradual build-up of effects such as those of word frequency. A single prior exposure to a low-frequency word can be sufficient to eradicate the comparative processing advantage normally enjoyed by a word of much higher frequency. Further problems for the recognition unit account of repetition priming are presented by the effects of repetition on *nonwords* in lexical decision tasks (Dannenbring & Briand, 1982; Scarborough et al., 1977). Since nonwords should not have logogens, a different basis for their facilitation must be postulated. It is clearly more parsimonious to account for repetition effects on both words and nonwords within the same conceptual framework.

There are thus clearly a number of problems for the traditional logogen interpretation of repetition priming effects with words. While some have attempted to surmount these problems by proposing (with some evidence) that there are both lexical and episodic effects operating in the usual priming experiment (e.g. Forster & Davis, 1984), others such as Jacoby and McClelland and Rumelhart have proposed more radical theoretical alternatives. Before considering these, let us consider equivalent evidence which proves difficult for "face recognition units."

In the last chapter, I described the results of a number of experiments on repetition and semantic priming of faces which seemed to be quite comfortably accommodated within a recognition unit framework. In particular, I described how Bruce and Valentine (1985) showed that repetition priming between two different views of the same person's face was not influenced by the degree of rated visual similarity between the two views. Now this always seemed to us an extremely odd result, given that visual similarity clearly did play some role in this task ... identical pictures produced more mutual priming than did different views of the same person. If there is an effect of identical picture matching, this should have given rise to some sort of graded visual similarity effect, due to a generalisation function, even if such an effect was weak.

One problem with Bruce and Valentine's method was that we, like Warren and Morton (1982) made use of a rather insensitive and post-hoc correlational technique in order to assess effects of similarity. As mentioned in the last chapter, recently A. Ellis et al. (1987) have reported an experiment in which they compared the amount of repetition priming produced in a face familiarity task by each of four experimental conditions: prior presentation of the name, a highly dissimilar picture of the face, a slightly different picture of the face, or an identical picture of the face. Like Bruce and Valentine, Ellis et al. found no effect of name priming, and the greatest effect for identical pictures. Unlike us, however, they found that slightly different pictures produced greater facilitation than highly dissimilar pictures. Thus their results were consistent with a visual memory, rather than a recognition unit effect (cf. Bruce, 1982, where I found recognition memory for unfamiliar faces was more impaired if both pose and expression were changed between presentation and test than if either pose or expression was changed).

A second line of evidence which is rather more easily accommodated by an instance-based than a recognition unit account is that relating to effects of distinctiveness in the recognition of familiar and unfamiliar faces (Valentine & Bruce, 1986b,c). In Chapter 3 I described how Tim Valentine has demonstrated that familiar faces rated as distinctive are more quickly recognised as familiar (as opposed to unfamiliar) faces, but more slowly recognised as faces (as opposed to jumbled faces) than are faces rated as typical in appearance.

A recognition unit account of the distinctiveness effect in the recognition of familiar faces would have to be cast in terms of signal-to-noise ratio. If a face is a typical face, its presentation will lead to partial activation in very many more recognition units than if the face is a distinctive face. To distinguish "actual" familiarity of a typical face (signalled by high activity within a particular recognition unit) from "apparent" familiarity (signalled by moderate levels of activity in numerous units) will require a more extended process of visual analysis than will be necessary for the distinctive face. The latter will therefore be recognised more quickly.

The recognition unit account copes less naturally with the effects of distinctiveness on the recognition of faces *as faces*. Current theoretical models differ in whether a separate "face classification" stage precedes the level of recognition units. Bruce and Young (1986) do not specify a stage within their model in which face classification occurs, and hence cannot really give an account of effects of distinctiveness in such a task. Ellis (1981; 1983; 1986a) suggests that faces are classified as faces before any further analysis leading to the extraction of semantic information. Such a model would attribute the effects of distinctiveness on face classification to a component different from that used to identify faces. It could be suggested that face classification (but not identification) was achieved by comparing an incoming pattern with a stored description of an average or "prototypical" face. Distinctive faces, by definition, look less like most other faces than do typical faces, and so would deviate from the stored prototype, making them more difficult to classify. Thus a model such as Ellis's could account both for the disadvantage of distinctive faces in a face classification task (through appeal to some comparison with a facial prototype), and for their advantage in a face familiarity task (through appeal to altered signal-to-noise ratio). This explanation is satisfactory, though somewhat unparsimonious.

A more economical explanation for the two "opposite" effects of distinctiveness can be achieved if we propose, as does Valentine (Note 7), that the internal representation of a face which allows us to recognise identity is coded in terms of deviation from an underlying facial prototype. As I described in Chapter 3, Valentine suggests that faces may be represented as vectors in a multidimensional space, with "dimensions" corresponding to psychologically significant variants of faces (e.g. sex, nose length, and hair colour could all be dimensions). The "prototypical" face would serve as origin for this space, and thus the vectors would represent deviations from this prototype.

A scheme such as this can readily explain the pattern of observed effects of distinctiveness, and provides a framework for interpreting face recognition which can readily accommodate caricature, for example (see Chapter 3). However, it begs the rather large question of where the "prototype," against which faces are compared, comes from in the first place. Although effects of prototypicality at first glance look as though they must result from some explicit abstractive mechanism, a number of instance-based accounts can account for such effects very well.

For example, Hintzman (1986) presents a model of long-term memory in which every episode is independently stored as a particular configuration of primitive properties (which are unspecified in the model), such that different experiences share some properties and differ on others. Memory is accessed via a "probe" item which results in an "echo" from long-term memory. The echo can vary in its *intensity* and *content*. The greater the similarity between the configuration of properties in the probe and stored traces, the greater the intensity, and hence the apparent *familiarity* of the event. The content of the echo reflects the summed contributions of all traces in memory, weighted by their similarity to the probe. If several traces are strongly activated, then the echo will reflect their *common* properties. "Prototype" abstraction can thus occur at retrieval, though no prototype has explicitly been abstracted and stored.

Hintzman's instance-based account thus sees prototypical effects emerging through retrieval processes. An account which appears to give very similar predictions, and which has recently been attracting much attention, is provided by the recent theory of McClelland and Rumelhart (1985).

DISTRIBUTED MEMORY MODELS

In 1981, McClelland and Rumelhart proposed an "interactive activation" model of word recognition, in which effects such as the word frequency effect were shown to be accounted for in terms of patterns of activation emerging from a network of simple units. The model comprised two main levels of feature detectors and word detectors, operating in "cascade," so that activity could begin at the word detector level before analysis at the feature level was completed. These different levels could both facilitate and inhibit one another, so that activity at the word detector level could affect that at feature detector level, and vice versa. We have already seen, in Chapter 4, how some kind of cascade system might be invoked to account for the "top down" influences of familiarity on judgements of the legality of a facial configuration (Bruce, 1986a), and have suggested that an "interactive activation" account of aspects of face recognition might prove fruitful.

However, McClelland and Rumelhart (1985) acknowledge the inconsistency in their earlier theory which sought to explain certain kinds of "abstractive" phenomena in terms of emergent properties, yet retained essentially abstractive units at the heart of the system. In their recent model, they seek to explain the apparently abstractive word detector units as resulting from storage of all instances of the word (or other concept) in question. Properties which look like those normally attributed to logogen-like units can be shown to emerge from a parallel distributed memory network which learns all instances of the concept. At the same time, memory for specific recent instances can be shown to be preserved within such a network.

The processing system in McClelland and Rumelhart's model consists of a network of simple processing units. Each unit is interconnected with very many other units, and the units communicate with each other by sending signals at strengths modulated by a corresponding set of weights. The units may be thought of as representing particular "features," whether of faces, of letters, or whatever, but McClelland and Rumelhart remark that features themselves may be encoded through patterns of activity within networks. The important point for us here is that the "primitive" elements of the system are not specified, and, as McClelland and Rumelhart note, the system requires an elaborate perceptual interface.

An important aspect of a memory model of this kind is that it is not really "instances" of concepts that are stored at all—what is stored are the weights between different connections, which change as a result of a particular instance. Memories are represented as patterns of activity in a "neural" net—patterns which can be recreated given partial activation of the network. A second important feature is that different concepts (different words, different faces, etc.) may be encoded by the same network simultaneously. Each processing unit contributes to the storage of all patterns processed by a particular module. Memories are not localised in discrete memory elements as they are in a digital computer, but are distributed across a large number of elementary units.

McClelland and Rumelhart's (1985) model is but one example of a "connectionist" model in which cognition is modelled as a changing pattern of activity in a network of units, rather than as the explicit construction and storage of abstract symbols. Not all connectionist models have distributed representations, however. In some models (e.g. Feldman, 1985), the units which are connected together represent discrete features or object concepts. It is the properties of distributed representations which hold most interest here. (However, it is worth noting that more recent attempts to model pattern recognition using multi-layered nets have incorporated "hidden units," where each hidden unit may come to represent some conjunction of local features in a more localised way [e.g. Hinton, Note 3].)

Connectionist models in general, and parallel distributed processing models in particular, have several properties which make them attractive as models of biological memory systems. Processing is massively parallel, and occurs via interconnected units which function in ways which resemble neurones. Performance in distributed systems is fairly robust if the system is "damaged" by removing some of the units.

McClelland and Rumelhart demonstrate the workings of a model of this kind by considering the behaviour of a simple information processing module, comprising a few processing units (they note that "real" modules would contain thousands or even millions of such units). The module receives input from, and sends output to, other (unspecified) modules for perception of the input pattern and appropriate action respectively. Each unit within the module can take on an activation level between -1 and $+1$, with 0 representing a neutral resting level, towards which activation levels will decay. Each unit is connected to all others within a module by a weighted connection.

During the first phase of each processing cycle, input to the module causes activity in all the units, which mutually affect one another's net activity according to the weightings in the connections. After all the activity for each unit has been summed, final activation levels are adjusted in the direction of the net input—thus positive activation levels become more positive and negative ones become more negative, though a decay factor will also operate against this. The consequence of all this is that on the next processing cycle, the internal inputs to any one unit will be slightly different, and so the net activities will alter, and so forth. A set of units is therefore in a dynamic state, but after a large number of cycles

(McClelland and Rumelhart use 50), there will be a stable pattern of activation over all the units.

Once the pattern has stabilised, adjustment of the weights on the connections between the units takes place. This is what constitutes "learning." A memory "trace" is the whole set of changes or *increment* to the weights of all the connections. The size and direction of the weight change at each connection is determined by *the delta rule*. This is a rule which moves the weights in a direction which makes the internal input to each unit (from all others in the network) tend towards that which matches the external input to that unit (from the stimulus pattern). The effect is to move towards a situation in which part of the stimulus pattern (affecting only some of the module's units) will lead to reproduction of the activity associated with the entire input pattern—cued recall. For example, if some of the units in a module are held to represent the visual form of the concept, and others to represent the name of this concept, after learning of the concept, the pattern associated with the name will be generated following presentation of the visual form alone.

Using their simple model module, McClelland and Rumelhart illustrate how the same module can be used to learn more than one distinct pattern, without any interference. Their module can learn the characteristics of hypothetical patterns corresponding to "bagels" at the same time as it learns patterns corresponding to "dogs". What is of most interest here, is what happens when the module learns a series of patterns which share a common structure, e.g. a series of dogs. McClelland and Rumelhart model this situation by presenting the module with a set of dog "instances," each of which is a stimulus pattern which is randomly distorted to a small extent from an underlying "dog prototype" (which the module is not exposed to during training). Following training with several such instances, the module will respond more strongly to the prototype pattern than to any distortion of it, but it will also respond strongly to patterns corresponding to the most recent instances in its training set. It has learned the prototype, while showing sensitivity to particular, recent instances.

What is interesting here is that we could conceive of such a module either as learning what characterises dogs in general, with each of the instances corresponding to different dogs (Fido, Rover, etc.), or we could think of it as learning the prototype of a particular dog (Fido), with each of the instances corresponding to different views of Fido on different occasions. The same principles will apply to the learning of exemplars of a particular item, as to exemplars of a particular category. What distinguishes the two cases is what information other than the stimulus pattern is encoded over the units of the module, since some subset of the units is given to encoding a "label" for each of the instances. Of particular interest is what might happen within a module which was exposed to several different instances of *each* of a set of different individual dogs—several different Fidos, several different Rovers, and so forth, along with information that each was an example of "a dog." I assume that such a module would learn general characteristics of individual dogs, as well as general characteristics of the concept "dog," but McClelland and Rumelhart's own simulation demonstrations did not extend to this situation. Such an extension is necessary to allow us to explain how the same module could learn about individual familiar faces, as well as about properties of faces in general. In Nottingham, Mike Burton and myself have just started simulation work of this kind.

McClelland and Rumelhart's model is just one example of a distributed model of memory which is currently attracting much interest. Other examples are contained in Hinton and Anderson's (1981) book, and in McClelland and Rumelhart (1986) and Rumelhart and McClelland (1986).

INSTANCE-BASED MODELS OF FACE RECOGNITION

The McClelland and Rumelhart system described here works on arbitrarily specified features or attributes, so its performance on real objects cannot be tested. A couple of neural net systems have been applied to faces, however, and in some respects they fare very well in recognising novel views of the individuals whose faces they have learned.

A system which has attracted much publicity for its apparently impressive performance on face recognition tasks is WISARD (WIlkie, Stonham and Aleksander's Recognition Device). WISARD is a general-purpose object recognition system which is based on neural net principles, implemented by massive dedication of memory to the storage of responses to instances of patterns on which it is trained (Aleksander, 1983; Stonham, 1986).

At one level, WISARD does not really constitute a distributed memory model, since it has a separate (i.e. localised) memory for each of the concepts on which it is trained. But its storage of each concept does result from the superposition of responses to a large number of instances—so at a more local level it is a distributed system. WISARD takes as its input an array of pixels, thresholded so that each pixel is either black or white. Random sets of n pixels are selected (where n is fixed for a particular application at some value between 2 and 8), so that the whole array of pixels is sampled. The results of this sampling process are stored in a memory bank, which is set up so that each possible result of taking an n-tuple sample addresses a distinct memory location. For example, if n is two, then for each of the pairs of pixels sampled, there are four possible outcomes: both pixels could be black, both white, the first black, or the second black. Each of these distinct possible outcomes has an associated memory location, at which either a zero or one may be stored, and each of the pairs of pixels sampled has its own such set of four distinct memory locations. At the start of training, all memories are set to zero, and then "ones" are stored at each address accessed by the samples from the first training pattern. If a different instance of the same concept is presented, and the same sets of pixels sampled, a slightly different pattern of responses will be recorded. Training on a particular concept (e.g. a particular person's face) involves repeating this process for a number of different instances and storing the responses in a "discriminator" (memory bank) devoted to this concept. Because of the statistical properties of particular objects, individual's faces, or whatever, some responses from samples will never occur if a pattern is a member of the concept, and others will always occur. In order to test the effect of training, a new instance of the concept can be given, and the number of logical ones accessed by sampling this new pattern can be expressed as a proportion of the maximum *possible* response strength. The maximum possible response would be achieved if every n-tuple sampled from a test pattern accessed an address where a "one" was stored. Training continues until the discriminator will reliably give about 95% of its maximum response when presented with novel instances of the concept.

If a number of different discriminators are each trained on different concepts, a system for classifying patterns is obtained. Thus if one discriminator is trained on Fred's face, one on Brian's face, and one on Harry's face, the system can be presented with new instances and asked to categorise them as one of the known people. The discriminator which gives the maximum response is the one which "wins" the decision. The WISARD system has been applied to faces in this way, and currently works well in recognising any one of 16 different individuals' faces, using an n-tuple size of 4, and an input resolution of 153×214 bits. About 200 different training images of each person are needed to get the system to give over 95% of its maximum response consistently to each individual. Provided that training is conducted over a range of different expressions, the system will classify new instances of the people regardless of their expression.

Because WISARD is a general-purpose system, it can learn to recognise any categories on which it is trained. Thus, just as it can learn to recognise an individual's face irrespective of its expression, so the system can learn to recognise an expression, irrespective of the identity of the person showing it. For example, the current system can learn to recognise a "smile" by having one discriminator trained on smiling faces and another on unsmiling faces (Stonham, 1986).

However, it is easy to be over-impressed by WISARD. It cannot do many of the things which humans find easy. For example, WISARD's performance will be critically dependent on the lighting conditions which prevailed during training, and will be unable to extrapolate to new views not encompassed by the training set. A WISARD trained on full-face views will never be able to recognise these people in profile. Nor is it obvious that the system could ever be trained to recognise *any* view of a face—it is not clear that the different views would have enough statistical overlap for such a system. Finally, WISARD currently distinguishes well between a set of 16 faces, but we can recognise hundreds of faces. It is not clear that a system of this kind could remain efficient as the number of similar concepts it is required to discriminate increases.

Nevertheless, the WISARD system is interesting. It demonstrates how storing the responses to large numbers of discrete instances of different people's faces produces something which looks like a set of face recognition units (albeit with limited powers to extrapolate to new views). Indeed, watching the performance of WISARD in real time very much gives the impression of watching a set of "resemblance detectors," as each discriminator signals the degree to which the responses to a test pattern resemble those stored during training. However, because WISARD is organised to have a separate discriminator for each known face, it is no better able to account for effects of distinctiveness than is the face recognition unit account.

Kohonen (1977; Kohonen, Oja, & Lehtio, 1981) has produced a distributed memory model, more closely related to McClelland and Rumelhart's than to WISARD, but which, like WISARD, works on real images, and has been applied to face recognition. Like McClelland and Rumelhart's model, Kohonen's assumes that learning of concepts may result from the distribution of different stimulus and response patterns across the same set of processing units. Within a module of such units, each unit is assumed to connect to all others, so that activation weights can be adjusted during learning. The response from a module reflects the summed activity of all the units—activity which is affected by the stimulus pattern currently active and by the weights that have been applied during learning.

Learning results from the adjustment of weights so that a particular stimulus pattern evokes a particular response. This weight adjustment occurs through the association of a stimulus pattern with a *forcing stimulus*, whose pattern is the same as that of the response required from the set of units. Thus a particular pattern of stimulation corresponding to the visual features of a dog might be associated with the forcing stimulus pattern corresponding to the label "dog," and the values of the weights altered so that, after learning, the stimulus alone will produce the required response "dog." This is where the system differs from McClelland and Rumelhart's, who make no distinction between "stimuli" and "responses" in terms of encoding—they arbitrarily allocate some of their units to the pattern of the dog, and others to the label.

The same network of units can be exposed to different stimuli and forcing stimuli and Kohonen has proved that, provided the training patterns are orthogonal (a mathematical property related to independence), a set of weights can be found so that each different stimulus pattern will prompt its appropriate response pattern with no contamination from the others encoded by the net. Even if the patterns are not orthogonal, Kohonen has shown that there is an approximative technique for fixing the values of the weights so that each stimulus pattern may be identified uniquely, even though the response output to each stimulus will not be identical to its associated forcing stimulus pattern.

Kohonen et al. (1981) demonstrated the properties of such networks using faces as examples of patterns with the kinds of statistical regularities which might produce interesting learning effects. In particular, using faces, they were able to show that a network of this kind would be able to generalise to classify correctly novel exemplars of learned stimulus categories. In one demonstration, a network of units was presented with the faces of 10 different people, each photographed in 5 angles ranging from a left $\frac{3}{4}$ view to a right $\frac{3}{4}$ view. These stimulus patterns were represented as the intensities (at one of 8 levels) in each of some 1200 input pixels. A distinct response was associated with the faces of each individual. Following this learning phase, the network retrieved the correct responses when presented with new examples of these faces—photographs taken at different angles from those of the original training set, though within the same range ($-45°$ to $+45°$). In each case the response pattern which resulted from the novel face was closer to the response which had been stored with other views of that individual than it was to any other of the stored responses. It would be interesting to examine whether effects of distinctiveness were found in this facial learning experiment. Presumably (though Kohonen has not examined this), those individuals whose faces resembled many others stored by the same network would produce responses which resembled those of other individuals more closely than would faces which were more distinctive.

Further interesting properties of this system result from *autoassociative learning*, where the forcing stimulus pattern equals the stimulus pattern. In this case, the network associates each stimulus with itself, and, given a partial or degraded stimulus pattern at test, will tend to reproduce the veridical stimulus pattern. In this case, the system is very similar to McClelland and Rumelhart's. Kohonen et al. (1981) again used faces to illustrate autoassociative learning effects, and show how a partial or degraded face can lead to the reconstruction of a complete face which has been learned by such a network.

Like the WISARD system, the Kohonen system is rather impressive in its ability to recognise novel interpolated views of faces without the construction of any explicit symbolic representation, but, like WISARD, it will show no capacity to extrapolate to novel views which depart much from the range on which it was initially trained. But the tests which Kohonen has run using faces should not be seen as definitive tests of such a model applied to face recognition. Rather, they are demonstrations of how the model performs with a convenient set of stimuli. As Kohonen et al. (1981) acknowledge, the visual system undoubtedly performs a number of preprocessing procedures on its input, which will result in some set of measurements more abstract than pixel intensity levels which such a net may encode. It is not legitimate to enquire about the adequacy of such a model as an account of human face recognition without incorporating such preprocessing procedures—we must, in other words, include a visual "front end" as well as a memory mechanism. In this respect, at this stage, McClelland and Rumelhart's demonstrations with hypothetical feature values varying from -1 to $+1$ are as important for our understanding of face recognition as are Kohonen's demonstrations using actual faces.

Millward and O'Toole (1986) present some suggestive evidence which is relevant here. They attempted to fit data obtained in a recognition memory task with the performance predicted by a Kohonen-style associative memory, and found a better fit to the model if it was based upon an encoding of the locations of oriented edge segments rather than "raw" pixel values. This result is interesting, but unfortunately their experiment confounded the nature of the representation that was input to the associative net with the number of pixels sampled in each condition. The memory simulations used only a subset of the pixels in the face images, and a larger patch of pixels was used to deliver the edge segment representations than was used in the raw pixel condition, so it could be this aspect which produces the superior performance. More work of this kind is clearly needed.

In the next chapter I will consider, within a computational framework, the nature of the features or other dimensions of faces which might be derived from facial patterns to drive networks such as these. Assuming such problems of encoding can be solved, what, if anything, is to be gained by this kind of framework over that developed in the last chapter? In the remainder of this chapter I discuss what I consider to be the possible advantages, disadvantages, and implications of a distributed memory approach to face perception.

IMPLICATIONS

A system such as McClelland and Rumelhart's can potentially accommodate certain aspects of face recognition more easily than an abstractive, "recognition unit" kind of approach.

Sensitivity to Recent Instances

Earlier in this chapter I reviewed A. Ellis et al.'s (1987) demonstration of graded effects of similarity in repetition priming in a face familiarity task. Likewise in "episodic" memory for familiar faces (Bruce, 1982), I showed faster response latencies to familiar faces if the same view was repeated at test compared with a different view. A distributed memory model of the kind developed by McClelland and Rumelhart (1985) can readily accommodate such effects. Although, in such systems, abstractive effects emerge from the superposition of all past instances, they can also demonstrate the retrieval of the precise pattern of the most recent instance. McClelland and Rumelhart (1985) provide numerous examples. The relative weight accorded to a recent instance will of course vary according to the way in which various parameters of the model are set—the important point is that both abstract ("structural") codes and specific recent instances can, in principle, be retained by the same network of units—allowing the potential integration of episodic memory for particular items (including faces) with initial identification of those items.

Effects of Distinctiveness

Effects of distinctiveness emerge quite naturally from the storage of patterns in a distributed memory network. Suppose a McClelland and Rumelhart type of network is presented with a set of "faces" which vary systematically around a hypothetical "average" face. For example, with a network of 12 units, each receiving an input of $+1(+)$ or $-1(-)$, the "faces" might be represented as $-+++----$, $+-++----$, $++-+----$, $+++-----$, $+++++---$, $++++-+--$, $++++--+-$, $++++---+$ (with a modal "average" of $++++----$), and the remaining 4 units might be devoted to storing a hypothetical pattern which corresponds to the categorical label, "face." If tested with the prototype of this set $(++++----)$, the response given by the units corresponding to the label will resemble that stored with the learned exemplars more closely than if the network is tested with an instance deviating from the prototype $(--++----)$. Assuming (nontrivially) that we can translate sensibly from response strengths in such simulation studies, to reaction times in error-free situations, this pattern mirrors that found by Valentine (Note 7) and Valentine and Bruce (1986c) in face classification tasks where subjects must distinguish intact from jumbled faces. As I noted in Chapter 3, subjects are faster to classify faces rated as "typical" than those rated as "distinctive."

I also noted in Chapter 3 that distinctive faces are *easier* to categorise as *familiar* than are typical faces, both in a face familiarity task involving highly familiar faces (Valentine & Bruce, 1986b,c; 1987) and in recognition memory for unfamiliar faces (Light et al., 1979). To simulate such results would require a rather more elaborate set of assumptions about the relationship between distributed memory models and particular task demands. We would need to set up a simulation in which a network was exposed to a series of individual "faces," each deviating to a greater or lesser extent from the "prototypical" face, but each given an individuating label. While we know already that such a network would give a stronger overall response to a "prototypical" than a distinctive face (cf. face classification), we would need to check that a particular partial "face" pattern led to more successful retrieval of its own individuating label the *less* it resembled other learned facial patterns. The latter task would be more analogous to that of face familiarity classification, where we must decide whether a given face is one of a particular, known individual, rather than just "a face" (i.e. the task is now to recognise a particular instance, rather than the abstracted properties of a class of stimuli). Clearly, while distributed memory models have much potential, they require further development and testing before they will naturally accommodate the data both from face classification and face familiarity tasks. The situation will become more complicated still when we allow the pattern corresponding to each individual's face to vary from instance to instance as well. It is at this point that simulation studies really become essential to the enterprise, as it becomes hard to predict the behaviour of such a system with more complex examples.

Context Effects in Recognition of Familiar and Unfamiliar Faces

In terms of the models developed, a "context" would be any other stimulus pattern which happened to be associated with the one in question. In McClelland and Rumelhart's model, we might construe contexts as forming part of the input pattern of units, or as activity in a different processing module with inputs to the units in question. In Kohonen's model, a context might operate as a "forcing stimulus," or again it might operate via a different processing module. These details need not concern us here (though they become crucial later on in the argument). What should concern us is that context could comprise any information associated with a particular face—place of encounter, clothes, associated faces, and so forth. Such an account could potentially allow a uniform treatment of context effects in episodic and identification experiments. However, there is no clear way, on such an account, to distinguish between the encoding and retention of some *contextual* event, and the encoding and retention of an item's semantic category or verbal label. This has some advantages compared with the treatment developed in the last chapter—it allows us to account quite neatly for the way in which certain acquaintances have "identities" which are equivalent to the contexts in which they are usually encountered—but it also poses some problems. The problems would come if we wished to draw a distinction between the relationship between a face and a semantic category, such as its owner's occupation (e.g. Stan Laurel is a comedian), and a face and its close associates (such as Oliver Hardy's face). One way around this problem may be to think about the different modalities through which different kinds of information are acquired (see the next section), which may affect the proposed modularity of a distributed memory system.

Creation of New Recognition Units

As I noted at the end of the last chapter, the "face recognition unit" account cannot readily deal with the question of when a face is familiar enough to have a special unit devoted to its perception. This is simply not an issue on a distributed memory account. If only a single instance of a face has been seen, then there will only be a single "trace" stored, which may be recognised again depending upon decay parameters, its deviation from other traces (i.e. its distinctiveness), and the deviation of the newly encountered instance from the original one (cf. Bruce, 1982). But if lots of instances of a particular face have been seen, then their common properties will be abstracted—producing something which looks like an abstracted set of "structural codes" for the item (see McClelland and Rumelhart's discussion of "logogens" in these terms). Apparent discontinuities in the processing of familiar and unfamiliar faces, such as the observed weight of processing devoted to internal features of familiar faces (see Chapter 3), could still emerge from such a system. A once-viewed still photograph of an unfamiliar face might be encoded with equal weight given to all features (to form what I have termed a "pictorial code" of such a photograph), but frequent encounters with faces might bias the representation towards internal features. External features are in some ways more variant over different instances, because of changes in hairstyle and paraphernalia, and we pay less attention to them in face-to-face interaction.

Derivation of Visually Derived Semantics Independently of Identity-specific Semantics

To the extent that sets of instances with intrinsic statistical similarities become associated with distinct categorical responses (cf. Kohonen), then we should, in principle, be able to recover from a particular novel instance of a face a range of visually derived semantic codes. Thus, for example, provided we have been told (perhaps explicitly, or perhaps indirectly via the processing of nonfacial information such as clothing) that some set of past instances are male faces and some other set are female, then a new face which has properties more in common with the average male face will be designated as male rather than female. Similar arguments could be applied to the categorisation of a face as young or old, oriental or caucasian, and even "looks like a popstar."

These kinds of argument allow us to make predictions with which to test such models. For example, the strength of a particular attribution should be some function of the number of instances in which we have been presented with an association such as "beautiful is good" (see Chapter 2). In Chapter 2, I noted recent work by Lewicki (1986a), in which he has shown how people may subconsciously learn associations between appearance and putative personality traits. Here I should also note that Lewicki (1986a) found that this effect was apparently *not* influenced by the number of such associated instances subjects encountered. Such results potentially challenge this account of the learning and retrieval of visually derived semantic codes, and further work of this kind, encompassing a broader range of variables, would clearly be of some interest.

Further problems for a distributed memory account of visually derived semantics may come when we try to accommodate stereotypical attributions such as "looks intelligent," "looks honest," etc., which have no apparent grounding in our history of facial instances. Here we must appeal to false instruction given by our family, friends, or by media portrayals of such categories as professors, criminals, and so forth (though we are still left without any account of the initial establishment of such culturally established, visually derived stereotypes).

Clearly, we have some way to go before a distributed memory account can offer a solution to all the problems posed by the kind of model developed in Chapter 4. Whatever the ultimate resolution of the distributed model's own possible difficulties in accounting for the derivation of identity-specific and visually derived semantic codes, such a model must in addition accommodate all the other evidence which the Bruce and Young framework was developed to handle. In the next section, I consider how such evidence may inform us of the modular structure of distributed memory systems.

MACROSTRUCTURE AND MICROSTRUCTURE

Although the distributed memory approaches seem to offer some possible resolution of problems raised in the last chapter, any such distributed memory account must also be able to accommodate the well-documented neuropsychological dissociations between different aspects of face processing, and also the sequential *dependencies* which have been demonstrated with normals. To recap; in Chapter 2 I reviewed evidence suggesting that expression analysis, facial speech analysis, and identification of faces are activities which appear to proceed independently of each other. An easy solution here might be to propose that expression perception results from the encoding of, say, facial action patterns, while identity perception is based upon encoding the permanent configuration of facial features, hairstyle, and so forth, so that the same processing module could quite easily accommodate these apparently independent categorisation processes. However, this is not quite sufficient to account for the apparent dissociation of expression perception and facial speech perception (Campbell et al., 1986; see Chapter 2), where we would expect the same information sources—facial action patterns—to drive the categorisation of both expression and facial speech. Clinical dissociations such as these probably force us to propose independent processing modules within a distributed memory system, which we could depict with discrete "boxes" in much the same way as shown in our original (Fig. 13) model.

Similarly, there is nothing intrinsic to a distributed memory model which allows us to explain easily why faces can never be named without the prior derivation of identity-specific semantic information. The relationship between identifying faces semantically and naming faces is again more easily accommodated by proposing some modular information-processing structure (much like that in Fig. 13).

Such considerations lead us to agree with Rumelhart and McClelland's (1985) claim that, in one sense, distributed memory models are models at a different *level* from models of the logogen kind. Distributed memory mechanisms may provide us with a mechanism for describing the *microstructure* of cognition—how things that look like abstractive "units" can emerge from a rather straightforward overlaying of independent instances—but we still require an understanding of the *macrostructure* of the processing modules which contribute to complex information-processing tasks. This point is important, and highlights the potential complementarity of the two approaches. The distributed memory approach gives us one possible way of getting "inside" the boxes we have drawn to indicate distinct functional components, and thereby providing a more detailed explanation of aspects of face processing. Considerations at the level of microstructure may, of course, have implications for the way in which we cast our macrostructural level theories, but the converse is also true. I anticipate that a profitable future direction for face research will arise from some combination of the macrostructural, modular approach derived by information processing theorists (Bruce & Young, 1986; Ellis, 1986a; Hay & Young, 1982), with a new distributed memory account of the microstructure of each of these modular components.

Let me conclude this chapter by presenting some thoughts about what such a system might look like. On the grounds outlined here, it is relatively easy to propose distinct modules for the analysis of facial speech, expression, and facial identification. Now we need a plausible account of the apparent modularity within the identification processes themselves. *Names* can quite plausibly be given a discrete module since they will be encoded in terms of a different set of parameters, and via distinct modalities. Names are either heard or read, and must be encoded and stored in terms of some combination of phonological and graphemic features. A similar argument may also serve for the encoding and storage of *semantic* information. Whether "visually derived" or "identity-specific," and whether essentially contextual or central to an item's meaning, semantic information will be *multimodal* in source, compared with the purely visual nature of facial patterns. As I said in Chapter 4, the "person identity nodes" in the Bruce and Young (1986) model were taken "outside" the cognitive system in order to emphasise the distinct role of identity-specific semantic information in the identification of familiar faces. We should think of these "nodes" as capturing one aspect of a vast store of semantic associations of various kinds—gained through combinations of visual, auditory, and other sensory experiences.

If faces are thought to be encoded in a module distinct from their semantics or labels because of the different modalities of the inputs to these modules, should the facial pattern module be thought of as storing the patterns corresponding to other visual objects too? My suspicion is that an account in which a distinct module is devoted to faces alone may provide a better account of evidence from clinical, developmental, and physiological sources, but for the moment I leave this question open.

These ideas are, of course, quite speculative. Further experimental and theoretical research, combined with simulation studies, will allow us to investigate the worth of such proposals. However, their potential merit will remain largely unexplored until we have some adequate theory of the nature of the visual parameters which are derived from faces and which may be encoded in memory: All the discussions of this chapter have been based upon the storage of hypothetical visual features (e.g. McClelland and Rumelhart's model) or on models which have used pixel intensity values as input (WISARD, and Kohonen's model). In the next chapter, I return to the question left hanging at the end of Chapter 3, and begged by all the subsequent discussion, about the derivation of the visual parameters which we use to distinguish between different faces.

6

Towards a Computational Theory of Face Perception

In the last chapter I described how an extension of work on instance-based memory systems could provide a potentially important way of improving upon our ideas of the microstructural components in models of face recognition. However, I also noted that such models are models of *memory* rather than of *perception*, and tell us nothing of the extraction of features, configurations, or whatever upon which the memory system may operate. It became clear towards the end of that chapter that, whether we retain our original "recognition unit" metaphor, or move to consider a distributed memory system, we must ultimately return to the question which we left dangling at the end of Chapter 3. What is the nature of the information which is encoded from faces which allows us to recognise them in different views and expressions? In the terms of Bruce and Young's (1986) framework, what are the "structural codes" for face recognition? In this chapter I will consider how a computational theory of face perception may eventually allow us to answer this question.

MARR'S THEORETICAL FRAMEWORK

The late David Marr left us with the richest recent theoretical framework for vision, within which we can begin to formulate questions specifically related to face perception. An important aspect of Marr's framework (Marr, 1982) was his specification of the different levels at which theoretical statements can be made. The "top" level of theory is a *theory of the computation* which the visual system must perform in order to solve some particular visual task (e.g. stereopsis). The theory of the computation specifies what it is that is being computed from the pattern of light on the retina, why this particular computation is being performed, and the nature of any constraints whose understanding may be brought to bear on the computation.

The next level is theory at an *algorithmic level*, in which the rules by which a computation can be effected are made explicit. Algorithms convert one representation into another. For example, Marr and Hildreth's (1980)

115

edge detection algorithm converts an initial array of brightnesses into a map of zero-crossings by convolving the original array with $\nabla^2 G$ (a filter which blurs the image with a Gaussian function and takes its second derivative with a Laplacian), and then setting all zeros to true and all nonzeros to false. Algorithms may conveniently be expressed as computer programs, in order to assess their performance on the task at hand. The third, and final, level of theory is the level of *implementation*, in neural tissue, electronic components, or whatever. Neurophysiologists and electronic engineers may be concerned with implementation level details; psychologists less so.

Marr stressed that algorithmic and implementation level theories must be guided by a theory at the computational level—a level at which the structures to be perceived are understood. It is this level of computational theory which has been missing from most research into face perception, and which I will emphasise in the first part of this chapter.

Before embarking on this task, however, it is worth summarising the theoretical framework for vision which Marr developed, since this too will have a bearing on face perception. On largely logical criteria, Marr identified four different stages of representation in vision, and specified some of the processes by which these representations could be constructed. The representation which forms the input to all later stages is *the retinal image*, which represents light intensities at different points in the image. Since changes in intensity potentially signal important boundaries in the viewed scene, the next set of processes operates on the retinal image to locate edges and regions. This results in the next representational level, *the primal sketch*, which describes the *two-dimensional* structures in the image.

The goal of early visual processing, according to Marr, is to describe the surface layout in the viewed scene. We need to relate the structures in the two dimensions of the primal sketch to shapes in the world. The representation which describes the distances and orientations of surfaces, relative to the viewer, is *the $2\frac{1}{2}D$ sketch*. Various different processes are seen as contributing to the construction of the $2\frac{1}{2}D$ sketch, including stereopsis, analysis of motion, recovery of shape from shading, and so forth. The $2\frac{1}{2}D$ sketch is a representation which allows the observer to orient him or herself to the structures in the world, but, according to Marr, view-dependent descriptions are inappropriate for the task of recognising the objects whose surfaces are viewed. On the grounds of parsimony, Marr suggested that object recognition must be mediated by view-independent descriptions, based on object-centred co-ordinate systems. The final representational level is therefore that of the *3D models*, which allow us to recognise the shapes of structures in the world from any viewpoint.

Marr's study of the recognition of natural objects (Marr & Nishihara, 1978) led to a representational scheme which, as we will see later in this chapter, does not naturally lend itself to the demands of face recognition. However, this representational scheme resulted from the more general argument that the goal of early vision is to describe *the three-dimensional shapes* of viewed structures. Now all the work which we described in Chapter 3 was based on the assumption that faces were 2D patterns, and that their structure could be described, both explicitly, and, by implication, internally, in terms of 2D measures. In Marr's terms, it is as though theories of face recognition have been based on the recovery and detection of structures in the primal sketch. But Marr's theory emphasises that the task faced by a viewer is to relate 2D image features to a model of the 3D surfaces and structures giving rise to these features. If we accept this position, then a perceiver viewing a face will, just as when viewing any other structure, represent the face as a *surface* with 3D structure. And, even if we did not wish to go so far as to suggest that the perceiver *represents* a face as a 3D surface (since we might suggest that "features" made explicit at a primal sketch level provide information sufficient for the perceiver's task), we still need to consider the nature of the object giving rise to such a 2D pattern, in order to comprehend the task faced by the perceiver. An example of this may be found in the work of Pearson (1986), who has been working on the problem of how to compress video images of human figures for automatic transmission to be used in video-phones for the deaf. To do this economically, it is necessary to compress the information into a line-drawing or "sketch." Pearson found that edge-detecting algorithms such as that used by Marr and Hildreth (described earlier) produced a representation which was cluttered with irrelevant edges. The contours which need to be located from an image of a face are those where the *surface* of the face slopes sharply away from the line of sight, as well as those arising from sharp intensity changes such as the hairline. Pearson and Robinson (1985) have developed an algorithm which can find both these kinds of contour, and, when it is applied to a facial image, the result is a line-drawing which looks remarkably similar to an artist's sketch of the face. Pearson's work thus demonstrates how understanding the nature of the face as a three-dimensional structure can have important consequences for the development of algorithms for facial processing. In the next section I consider the nature of face structures in some detail.

FACES AS SHAPES

Marr has provided us with numerous examples of how the constraints of the physical world may be exploited by a viewer trying to make sense of images of that world. For example, in his work on the derivation of the primal sketch (Marr, 1976), Marr pointed out how the coherence of physical matter and the generally smooth shapes of natural objects provide constraints which can be exploited in the perceptual organisation of different parts of an image. In work on stereopsis, Marr and Poggio (1976; 1979) showed how the spatial localisation of objects, and the relative rarity of abrupt changes in depth (and hence disparity) could be used to constrain the solution of the problem of correspondence between the disparate images received by the two retinas. Other work by Marr pointed out general properties of particular classes of objects, such as those comprised of generalised cones (Marr & Nishihara, 1978). (Generalised cones are elongated shapes which result from sweeping along an axis a cross-section of constant shape but variable diameter: vases and rugby footballs are examples. Many natural shapes, such as animals, are made of parts which approximate to generalised cones.) When we consider the particular problem of perceiving faces, there may also be important lessons to learn by considering the nature of the structures to be viewed *before* we suggest ways in which these structures may be represented internally, and algorithms for the derivation of these representations.

The first consideration which we can bring to the study of facial structures is the realisation that faces *grow* on *heads*. Figure 15 shows an infant skull, scaled up in size, beside an adult skull. Notice the changes which growth has produced, and the consequences that such changes have for the "soft" facial structures appended to such skulls. The infant forehead is proportionately much larger, and its lower face (nose and chin) much smaller than the adult's. The process of growth involves a global

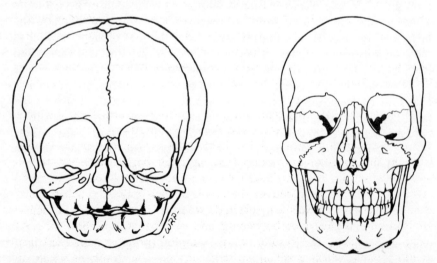

FIG. 15. The skull on the left is an infant's skull, scaled up in size to equal the adult's skull shown on the right. Notice the complex change in the shape of the skull as the child grows. Reproduced from Enlow (1982), with permission of author and publishers.

transformation in the overall head structure, and different parts of the face/head shape contribute in an *interdependent* rather than an independent fashion.

The American orthodontist Enlow (1982) has described the nature of the structures produced by these interdependent growth processes. He describes different facial "types" in which certain characteristics co-vary. The two extreme forms of head shape are the dolichocephalic (long, narrow) head form, and the brachycephalic (wide and short) head form; according to Enlow, these extremes of head form give rise to corresponding extremes of facial type—the leptoprosopic (long, narrow, and protrusive) and the euryprosopic (broad and less protrusive). In Fig. 16 is Enlow's illustration of how facial characteristics are constrained by the underlying head shape.

The dolichocephalic head form gives rise to a face in which the eyes are relatively close set, the nose is long, thin, and protrusive, with a high bridge, and often with a convex profile shape. Because of the protrusive nose, the part of the forehead immediately above the eyes and nose will be

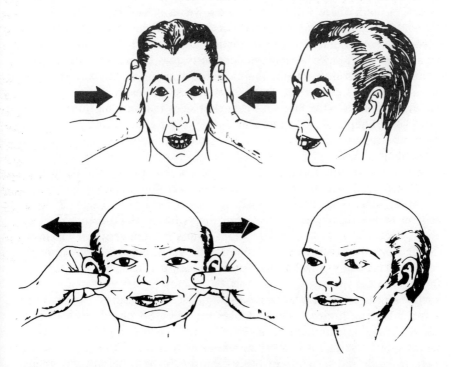

FIG. 16. Dolichocephalic (top) and brachycephalic (bottom) heads produced as though the head form were squeezed inwards (top) or stretched outwards (bottom). Reproduced from Enlow (1982) with permission of author and publishers.

R.F.—I

more prominent, and the forehead slopes back. The leptoprosopic face is therefore narrow and angular. The euryprosopic face, in contrast, is flat. The eyes are wide set, and the nose is short, wide, and often concave in profile. The cheekbones appear to be higher than in the leptoprosopic face.

Of considerable interest is Enlow's observation that the differences which characterise these two basic head types bear some relationship to the differences between infant (wide and flat) and adult (long and narrow) faces, and female (wide and flat) and male (long and narrow) faces. The reasons for the relationships are the same in all cases. According to Enlow, one of the determinants of the head/face shape is the size of the nose, which is determined by the requirements of the body. Infants, and females, have relatively smaller bodies and lung capacities, and thus require relatively smaller nasal chambers than do adults and males.

What is the relevance of these observations for our understanding of face recognition? The first lesson we can learn is that theories of face representation which treat faces as lists of independent parts are unlikely to be very relevant to our perception of real faces, in which the parts themselves may be impossible to delimit (Where does the nose "begin"? Is a chin a "part"?), and where the parts have grown in a way in which they are dependent upon one another and on the underlying head structure. A second lesson is that face reconstruction devices such as Photofit, which treat faces as "jigsaws" of independent parts, may be unsuccessful, in part, because the features are not mutually constraining in the way that real facial features are. For example, according to Enlow, a short, pug nose should go with a wide face and wider-set eyes than a long thin nose. In Aberdeen, Shepherd, Ellis, and Davies (1977) have factor-analysed a large number of measurements made on a reasonable sample of photographs of adult male faces, and revealed factors which suggest very strongly that certain facial features go together with others. The first two of the factors which emerged from their analysis both revealed this redundancy (Factor 1: large, wide, open face vs. small, narrow, closed face; Factor 2: long, narrow face with thin features vs. short, wide face with fat features). Note that Factor 2 in particular looks very reminiscent of Enlow's dolichocephalic-brachycephalic dimension. It would be interesting to repeat such a study of facial variation using measurements made of the face in three, rather than two, dimensions, to get more satisfactory measures of such features as the nose. Even without such 3D measures, the relationships between different facial features found by Shepherd et al. (1977) could clearly be exploited in an "intelligent" electronic photofit system, which might use features that the witnesses feel they have remembered well, to guide the selection of other features likely to belong with them. And it may be that the police artist achieves superior performance over the various "kits" in part because of some implicit knowledge of facial structures which can be brought to bear upon the drawing. A final, and most important lesson, is that the information which we extract from faces, and which forms the basis for our "structural codes" for faces, may reflect the constraints within these shapes. If dimensions of facial variation can be described formally in terms of a relatively small number of global parameter variations, perhaps observers encode faces in terms of these parameters.

Such insights are not new, and work on the nature of global parameters to which we may be sensitive when viewing faces has already been started within the framework of ecological optics. Bob Shaw and his associates (e.g. Pittenger & Shaw, 1975; Shaw, McIntyre, & Mace, 1974) began work into the perception of ageing which has revealed the mathematical nature of the transformation from infant to adult. Most of this work has been conducted on 2D outlines of skull profiles, but, as we will see, the work readily extends to 3D.

The shape of the profile of a human head is rather like an inverted heart structure with a rounded top—a *cardioid* (see Fig. 17). Shaw et al. (1974) showed how a cardioidal *strain* transformation could be applied to the outline skull of a year-old infant to map it onto the skull profile shape of a

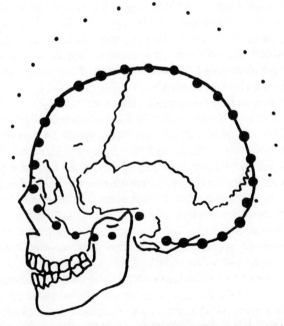

FIG. 17. The small dots show a regular cardioidal shape lying above a profile of a human skull. Appropriate transformation of this shape gives a good fit to the shape of the skull. From Shaw et al. (1974). Copyright © 1974 by Cornell University. Used with permission.

10-year-old and a 25-year-old. Growth as cardioidal strain makes sense given the stresses imposed on the bones of the skull by the growth of softer tissues. Pittenger and Shaw (1975) and Mark and Todd (1985) have obtained evidence that a strain transformation is much more successful in accounting for perceived age differences than is a shear transformation.

The 2D cardioidal strain transformation used by these workers can be expressed in polar co-ordinates as: $R' = R(1 - k\cos \theta)$, $\theta' = \theta$, where k is a free parameter increasing over time (the larger the value of k, the greater the age transformation). Mark and Todd (1983) have described how expressing the algorithm in spherical co-ordinates allows its application to 3D shapes: $R' = R(1 - k\cos \theta)$, $\theta' = \theta$, $\phi' = \phi$.

In deriving these equations they incorporated their finding that the effects of gravitational stresses on growth apply equally in all vertical planes passing through the central axis of the head, and hence the age transformation is only a function of θ, the angular elevation or "latitude" of a point on the surface, and is not affected by ϕ, the "longitude." In order to explore this possible extension to 3D, Mark and Todd (1983) went to the extraordinary length of producing computer-sculpted busts of an original and a younger version of a girl's head. The teenaged girl was photographed by the Solid Photography Studio, using a process for optical digitisation of a solid object. This results in a database for the head in 3D, and this database was then used to cut a bust of the girl in plastic using a computer-driven lathe. The original database was then age-transformed in a direction which should have produced an apparently younger child ($k = -0.2$), and a second bust was cut from the transformed database. The two busts are shown in Fig. 18.

These two busts were then shown to observers who were unfamiliar with the particular child, and they were asked to estimate the age levels of each of them. The "older" bust was given a mean age of 14.5 years (S.D. 1.5) and the "younger" bust a mean age of 6.3 years (S.D. 0.9). At the time when the bust was made, the child was actually aged 15 years, and parents and siblings judged the "younger" bust to resemble the child at about 5 years of age. These results are even more remarkable given the comments of these relatives of the absence of "baby fat" from the age-transformed bust. Mark and Todd's (1983) research thus convincingly validates the ageing algorithm as applied to the natural three-dimensional forms of heads.

What is the relevance of the discovery of the cardioidal strain transformation to theories of the perception of faces? The work has demonstrated that perceivers are sensitive to the transformational level of an underlying cardioidal shape, and can use this to assess both relative and absolute age levels in faces. Thus the transformational status of the shape specifies age. However, it has also been shown that the individual identity of a particular

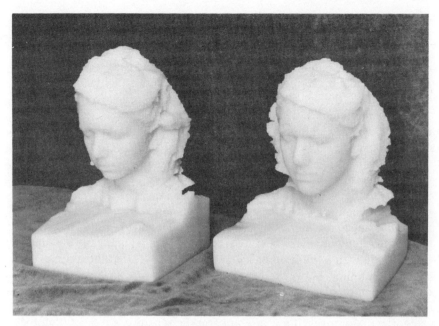

FIG. 18. The two busts used in Mark and Todd's (1983) study. On the right is the original bust of a girl aged 15 years, and on the left is shown the bust which resulted from transforming the original head using three-dimensional cardioidal strain to make the head look younger. Reproduced with permission of the authors, and the Psychonomic Society.

profile can be preserved despite the age transformation. Pittenger and Shaw (1975) showed that subjects were quite successful at matching a particular skull outline against the appropriate member of a pair transformed to a different age level.

There is other, compelling evidence that perceivers may be sensitive to this kind of global parameter variation between faces. First, the Aberdeen group has demonstrated that the major dimensions which seem to account for perceived variations between faces are those of hairstyle, *face shape, and age* (Shepherd et al., 1981). Second, Fagan and Singer (1979) have provided a fascinating demonstration of the apparent sensitivity of infants to these kinds of global parameters. In a number of experiments using a habituation paradigm, Fagan and his colleagues have demonstrated how infants' powers to distinguish between faces develop over the first seven months of life. We know from a number of studies that very young infants prefer face-like to nonface patterns (Goren, Sarty, & Wu, 1975), but it is not until the infant is five or six months of age that he or she can distinguish male from female, or old from young faces, and the ability to distinguish between individual male or female faces is not shown until about the age of seven months. (I am here referring to memorial discrimination between faces which are novel to these infants, who may be able at a much younger age to recognise the faces of their particular caretakers, and whose powers of perceptual discrimination may be underestimated by the habituation memory paradigm.) Now this pattern of development might, at first glance, seem to reflect the specificity of the information needed to make each of these different kinds of distinction between novel faces (cf. Sergent, 1986). However, Fagan and Singer (1979) tested 5–6 month-old infants on their ability to distinguish between faces in terms of their age, sex, or identity, with surprising results. These babies could distinguish between two faces of widely different age, but similar features (the face of a middle-aged, bald, fat man and the face of a baby), or between two faces of different sex which had similar features (the faces of a brother and sister of similar age and hairstyle), but could not distinguish between two male faces, or two female faces with highly dissimilar features (e.g. the bald, fat man, and a younger, thinner man with a full head of hair). It thus appears that these infants are not distinguishing between the sex or age of faces in terms of highly distinctive, particular features, but are using much more subtle information about the overall configurations which distinguish these different categories. Moreover, they are apparently sensitive to these "global" variations before they show evidence of sensitivity to particular, "local" properties.

The work on ageing, described here, has pointed to a possible "global" parameter which may be used to make age judgements. Can we describe in formal terms the differences between the leptoprosopic and euryprosopic facial types, or between male and female faces? According to Enlow (1982), these types result from different head shapes which bear some resemblance to the infant and adult head shapes, so it is possible that similar global transformations might apply. In Nottingham, we have recently started work in which we will experiment with the effects of different global shape transformations on the perceived properties of synthetic 3D head models. It is hoped that this work will lead us to a better understanding both of the nature of 3D head structures *per se*, and to further understanding of the information which may be extracted and stored in facial recognition . . . the importance of configural information in face perception may stem, in part, from its use in determining variations in face shape, sex, and age of faces.

An important future direction for such work would involve suggesting *algorithms* for the extraction of such information about facial variation. The work on ageing does not address this question, since it has been cast within a noncomputational framework. But those of us who adopt an information-processing framework need to know *how* information is detected, not just *what* is detected. Thus we must ultimately address the question of what algorithms operate to convert an image of a face into a representation of a face suitable to subserve its recognition. In the next section I make some suggestions about the kind of representational framework which might prove useful for considering the "how" of facial processing.

REPRESENTATIONS FOR RECOGNITION

In order to recognise a particular visual pattern as belonging to a particular category of object (where object categories might be rather general—a dog—or fairly specific—my husband's face), we must match the incoming pattern against a representation of that category which has previously been stored. One way to explain how we recognise novel instances of objects in a range of different angles, lightings, and so forth, is to suggest that we match an incoming pattern against a collection of instances stored of all our previously encountered views of the object. The WISARD system which I described in the last chapter is an extreme example of such a system. Such a system uses a form of representation based upon the image itself, an extreme form of *viewer-centred* co-ordinates, and will require separate storage of items at different distances or locations in the field of view, as well as of different angles, expressions (in the case of faces), and so forth. In contrast, representations based upon a co-ordinate system intrinsic to the object itself will be more complex to derive, but will provide for less redundant storage. In the extreme, an object recognition system of the kind proposed by Marr and Nishihara (1978) requires that only a single representation need be stored for each object category known, which can be accessed from any viewpoint.

A face is a naturally elongated object, with some key features, such as the eyes and mouth, which might be used to establish a canonical frame of reference for the representation of its specific details, at least from views which do not depart too much from full face (note that Perrett et al., 1984; 1985; find certain "face specific" cells in the brains of monkeys to be dedicated exclusively to profiles, and it is possible that these might require representation via a rather different canonical frame). The suggestion that faces are represented in an *object-centred* co-ordinate system does not necessarily imply that a single representation is stored for each face—different views and expressions might still be represented discretely—but a canonical co-ordinate frame would allow the visual system to treat as equivalent the same face at different viewing distances (within limits) or at different places within the field of view (within limits).

What might be the primitives of such a representation of a face? Marr and Nishihara (1978; see also Nishihara, 1983) argue for *volumetric* primitives in the description of certain classes of natural shapes which have the approximate shapes of *generalised cones*. Thus they propose that the shapes of animals be described in terms of the spatial arrangement of the axes of their component generalised cone parts. A "human" would be distinguished from a "gorilla," for example, by the relative lengths of the axes corresponding to the arms and legs. They also suggest a possible means of deriving such an axis-based representation, based upon analysing the occluding contours in images of these objects.

The Marr and Nishihara scheme is attractive, since it allows shape representations to be organised in a modular fashion, with descriptions at a global level giving the overall shape of the trunk and limbs of an animal, with pointers to detailed descriptions of local components such as the fingers of the human hand. However, as argued elsewhere (Bruce & Young, 1986), it is not a suitable scheme for face recognition, since all faces have similar overall three-dimensional structures, in terms of the volumetric primitives they propose.

Pentland (1986), however, has outlined a more flexible volumetric scheme in which complex shapes are seen as composed of *superquadrics*. Superquadrics are a very general class of shapes which include all basic types such as spheres, cylinders, or cubes, and allow these to be bent, twisted, or otherwise deformed and combined with one another to produce an infinite variety of complex man-made and natural shapes. Figure 19 shows a human face built of superquadric components. Pentland has built this face with a set of 13 primitives. The head shape itself is a slightly tapered ellipsoid, with the addition of features made from other basic shapes—the nose is a kind of cuboid shape and the ears are pancake-like shapes, and so forth. Pentland suggests that a particular face could be represented in terms of the particular variations of the shapes of its component parts, and their relationships. The possibility of building faces out of such volumes is intriguing, and certainly Bridgman's (1924) pre-scriptions for drawing faces look very like Pentland's synthetic technique (see Fig. 20). But a major drawback of such an approach is that it does not naturally allow the specification of surface details, which we know carry vital information for face recognition, and it may be difficult to assimilate the apparent effects of global transformations, as in ageing, to such an essentially discrete representational format.

An alternative direction for the representation of faces might be given by a *surface-based* representation. Mark and Todd's (1983) application of the ageing transformation to a 3D head model operated via such a surface-based representation, and Parke (1982) and Baker, Hogg, and Lloyd (Note 1) have used such surface-based facial representations for their applications in computer animation and medical imaging respectively. The shape of the face may be approximated by a multifaceted set of polygons,

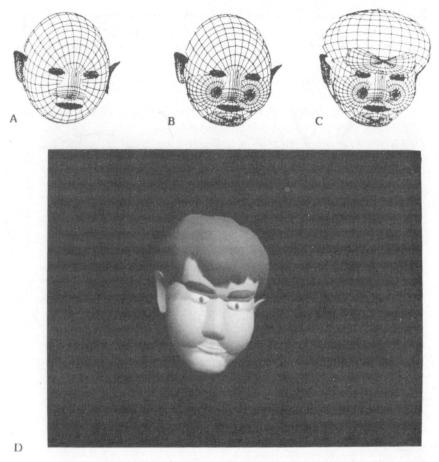

FIG. 19. A head built from superquadric components. Reproduced from Pentland (1986) with permission.

as shown in Fig. 21. Such a representation allows the application of *global* deformations (as in ageing, cf. Mark & Todd, 1983) as well as *local* surface changes. Local parts can easily be specified by "marking" a portion of the surface for special treatment. An intriguing possibility here would be to examine whether we can produce three-dimensional caricatures (cf. "Spitting Image" models) by extending the ideas of Brennan (see Chapter 3) to such a three-dimensional surface representation.

What is the relevance of these representational schemes which have proved useful in the *synthesis* of face models to our understanding of possible internal representations? Clearly we would not want to suggest that the human brain itself constructs a multifaceted polygon. But the

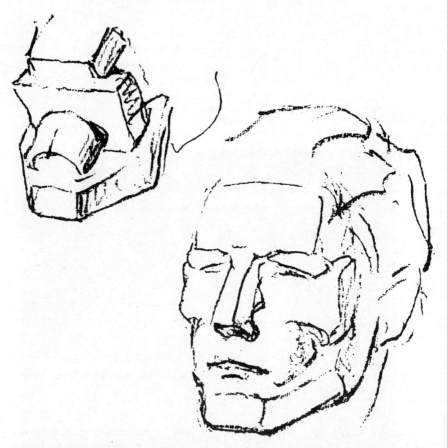

FIG. 20. Examples of Bridgman's prescriptions for life drawing. Note how Bridgman sees the face as comprised of solid volumes. Reprinted by permission of Sterling Publishing Co., Inc., Two Park Avenue, New York, NY 10016 from "Bridgman's Complete Guide to Drawing From Life" © 1952 by Sterling Publishing Co., Inc.

visual system might construct a symbolic description of the relative orientations of different parts of a surface, which we could think of as representing the directions pointed by normals to planes tangential to different surface "patches." Marr (1982) gives a good introduction to such "gradient space" representational formats which have proved useful in building descriptions of surface orientations in other domains.

How might such a 3D surface description be derived, in principle, from a natural image of a face? Let us assume that a facial pattern is encoded initially as a 2D variation in light intensity, and the structure of this 2D image is then made explicit in the full primal sketch (Marr, 1976)—which should reveal important occluding contours such as the overall face outline,

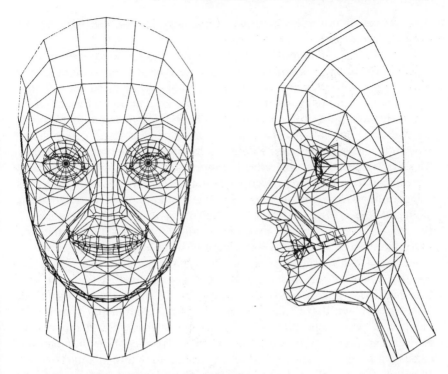

FIG. 21. A multifaceted polygon model of the surface of the face. From Parke (1982), reproduced with permission. Copyright © 1982 IEEE.

the outline of the hair, and of facial features, along with surface features such as wrinkles and blemishes. Now locating facial features reliably from a 2D image representation is a far from trivial problem (cf. Craw, Ellis, & Lishman, 1987), so a purely "bottom-up" derivation of the full primal sketch will rarely contain a really "clean" description of these different parts. It is possible that grouping procedures might be supplemented by top-down influences using knowledge of the general configuration of facial features. The fact that minutes-old infants show reliable preferences for face-like patterns suggests that a very general face "model" may be innate, and the suggestion that the processing of faces may involve "top-down" guidance at a computationally early stage would both simplify the computational procedures and allow an explanation for the "hollow face" illusion, which I discuss later. The next stage would be to combine the analysis of the image in 2D with the building of a description of the surface thus depicted. This will involve the derivation of the shape of the face from patterns of contour and shading, and when viewing natural faces, information from stereopsis and motion might also contribute (see Marr, 1982, for descriptions of possible algorithms for computing surface structure via these different routes).

What evidence is there that people use any of these sources of information to derive a representation of the facial surface in three, rather than two dimensions? Certainly the fact that we recognise faces so readily from static photographs suggests that stereoscopic and motion information are relatively unimportant sources of information for recognition purposes. But we are good at recognising photographs of all sorts of other objects too, in the absence of accurate depth or motion information. It seems that for object recognition generally, stereopsis and motion are not *necessary* for the building of shape descriptions suitable for recognition purposes. Johansson (1973) has demonstrated that information from motion patterns alone may be *sufficient* to specify certain *basic-level* object categories. If the joints of an otherwise invisible moving actor are illuminated, one immediately sees the display as being a moving human figure. However, more detailed discrimination about the sex of the walker, or his or her identity, takes longer, and is much less accurately perceived (Cutting & Kozlowski, 1977; Kozlowski & Cutting, 1977). Similarly, Bassili (1978; 1979) has shown that if the surface of a face is illuminated with a large number of points, the face is easily seen *as a face* when it moves, and subjects can decide, well above chance, which facial expression the motion corresponds to, a result we have replicated in Nottingham (Bruce & Valentine, in press). In Nottingham we also explored whether subjects would be able to perceive the identities of their colleagues in displays such as these. Subjects were told the names of the six possible highly familiar people whose faces would appear. While performance with the moving point-lit faces was above chance, and superior to that obtained from static views of the same displays, it was far from accurate.

The conclusion we draw from this work is that, in the absence of "static" cues about configuration, motion can provide sufficient information to specify that the surface is a face (rather than some other object) and some information which can help determine the identity of the face (though much less reliably). Motion can provide sufficient information to specify "a face" but rather little about "whose face." When good configurational cues are present (as in a photograph), motion probably provides redundant information, and this may explain why recognition memory experiments rarely demonstrate an advantage of dynamic vs. static presentation or test modes (Patterson, 1978; Shepherd, Ellis, & Davies, 1982; Bruce & Valentine, in press; though see Schiff, Banka, & Galdi, 1986, who did find an advantage for "dynamic" mugshots).

The role of stereoscopic depth information in face perception has not been systematically explored, but it seems unlikely to be an important one. The "hollow face" illusion (Gregory, 1973) (in which a facial "mask" is seen as a real face, with its nose pointing towards us) shows how stereo-scopic, and motion, information can apparently easily be ignored when we view faces. Only when we are very close to the mask does stereopsis "win" and force us to see its hollow shape. The illusion also provides some tentative evidence for the importance of shading routines in face percep-tion, since there are no surface markings to help locate the features present in the mask. Although luminance changes are present at creases, etc., it seems to be the whole pattern of shading information which helps reveal the "face" in such a mask. The effectiveness of cosmetics in altering apparent face shape, and the careful use of lighting in the production of stage photographs, also suggest that information in patterns of shading contributes to our perception of facial appearance. This suggestion about the importance of shape from shading in face perception is bolstered by the evidence that recognition of faces from line drawings, even when quite detailed, is much poorer than from photographs (Davies et al., 1978b). Good sketch artists add a lot of information about shading to their drawings. Finally, note that Benton and Gordon (1971) found a positive correlation between the ability to discriminate patterns of shading and face recognition ability. Of course, as we noted in Chapter 3, caricatures provide better representations for identification purposes than do unex-aggerated line drawings of the same individuals (Rhodes et al., in press). Perhaps this is because, in the absence of good veridical information about the configuration of the face as a surface, it is better to exaggerate (and hence highlight) the distinctive aspects of the 2D information remaining.

I would therefore argue that information derived through the analysis of shape from shading will be more important to the derivation of a descrip-tion of face shape than information from other visual processing modules such as stereopsis or motion. This is not to deny any role for these other sources, which may be revealed when other cues are absent, but merely to suggest that motion and stereo may usually provide redundant informa-tion.

Once a description of the surface of the face, and its markings (which may be used to "delimit" portions of this surface, such as the eyes or lips) is built up, what next? So far, I have assumed that the representation of a particular view has been derived. The next stage may then involve a conversion to object-(face-)centred co-ordinates. Such a representation might then be used to derive a more abstract symbolic description of the face, suitable for recognition purposes, in which the face is described by variations in a number of *parameters*. A relatively coarse-grained descrip-tion may suffice to specify the overall face/head shape, approximate age level, and perhaps to specify configurational information allowing us to tell the sex of the face (cf. Sergent, 1986). Local details may also be made explicit so that finer distinctions can be made, and so that we can recognise faces from partial information. Surface markings will also be made explicit—and may provide important cues about the precise age, sex, and identity of the face. An actor can be made to look older or younger without any alteration of his facial configuration—adding or removing wrinkles can be remarkably effective. In these terms, a representation of a face comprises measurements of a number of different global and local shape parameters along with details of surface markings. Note that I have not given any suggestions about how parameters may be derived, only about how a detailed surface-based representation might be derived. It might be that the parameters themselves emerged from the distributed representation of a large number of faces, each encoded in the kind of co-ordinate structure I have proposed, through the attunement of hidden units. The important point is that we will not be able seriously to test the relative merits of an "abstractive" or "instance-based" system for the storage of invariant information characterising individual faces, or groups of faces (e.g. old faces, female faces) until we have developed good ideas about the representational systems from which such invariants may be derived.

Where do the arguments given in this chapter leave all the experimental evidence described in Chapter 3? As I have already indicated, research which stresses the different roles played by information at different spatial scales (e.g. Sergent, 1986) is accommodated quite naturally within a computational framework. My position is that a "complete" theory of facial representation will combine the insights gained from considering the underlying 3D structure of the head, and possible representations of it, with some of our knowledge of configural and feature properties derived from treating faces as 2D patterns, which we considered earlier. Ignoring the nose, a full-face view of a face is approximately planar, so working on the properties which are defined in the full-face view, and treating this as though it were a "flat" structure, will not necessarily produce misleading results in our experiments. However, I noted in Chapter 3 that the relative unimportance of the nose in studies of feature saliency may be distorted by the emphasis on full-face patterns in which the nose is poorly specified. The fact that so much cosmetic surgery involves alterations to the nose, and that the results of such surgery may have dramatic effects on the impression created by the face, illustrate that the nose is far from unimportant in real life. It may be that the apparent advantage for $\frac{3}{4}$ views of unfamiliar faces (reviewed in Chapter 5) may stem in part from the better description of the surface shape available from such a view. For familiar faces, such an advantage may be off-set by our frequent experience of full-face views, given their importance in face-to-face interaction. What I am suggesting here is that we *supplement* the results obtained from considering faces as flat patterns, with a more careful analysis of what these results mean, in terms of a theory of representation of faces. My suggestion here has been that faces may be represented in terms of a combination of global and local parameters derived from a representation of the surface of the face, combined with the analysis of occluding contours and surface markings available from the 2D image of a face. Further specification of these parameters, and suggestions about how they may be derived from a surface description, are fruitful topics for further psychophysical and computational experiments.

CONCLUSIONS AND IMPLICATIONS

The last two chapters of this book have been fairly speculative, and are intended to point to directions which may shape our theories of face recognition in years to come. Whatever the ultimate fruitfulness of these latter suggestions, this book as a whole has described the attempts of cognitive psychologists to specify an information-processing framework for face recognition. Within such a framework, the recognition of faces of friends and celebrities can be seen to result from a number of distinct and complex visual and cognitive components. Such a framework makes our usual success at recognising familiar faces all the more remarkable, and perhaps makes our occasional errors comprehensible. I will conclude this book by returning briefly to problems of witness testimony raised in Chapter 1, and considering what we have learned which may be of application in this context.

A number of findings discussed within this book have potential implications for the way in which we question witnesses, and indeed many recommendations have already been made as a result of such research. For example, the susceptibility of face recognition memory to interference from large numbers of distractor faces (Laughery et al., 1971; see Chapter 1) makes it inadvisable for witnesses to look through many hundreds of faces in a file of "mug-shots." The Aberdeen group (e.g. see Shepherd, 1986) has developed an automatic means of limiting the number of photographs to be examined by making use of an initial witness description to access a set of mug-shots fitting this description, which the witness may inspect. A further example is given by the possible beneficial effects of reinstating context (see Chapter 4), which would lead us to suggest that, wherever possible, contextual reinstatement and/or "guided memory" techniques should be used when faces are to be recognised or described (Davies, 1986, provides a review). Davies and Milne (1985), for example, found that both guided memory techniques and actual contextural reinstatement (returning witnesses to the room in which an incident occurred) helped witnesses to make more accurate Photofit constructions of target faces, and there was also a trend (though nonsignificant) for recognition of the target face to be improved.

An area which seems to me to hold much potential for future application of our theoretical ideas is in the refinement of reconstructive kits, like the Photofit. The current slow, manual selection of facial features from a physical kit will rapidly be replaced with electronic Photofit systems, in which faces may be constructed interactively and features altered and blended in subtle ways. As we learn more about the way in which faces are represented, so we should be able to improve such systems, and find ways of overcoming their limitations. For example, the demonstrations of con-figural processing described in Chapter 3 show how quite the wrong overall impression could be gained from correctly remembered features placed in a context of others which are wrong (e.g. see Fig. 8). One lesson to be learned here is that a witness should always work with a whole facial configuration, rather than with parts of it, but the witness may also be encouraged to try concealing top or bottom halves at times in order to check whether more local impressions fit their memory. We may also be able to improve upon the accuracy of poorly remembered features if we can incorporate knowledge of constraints between different features, as suggested earlier in this chapter. As well as allowing for the possible development of "intelligent" electronic Photofit systems, knowledge about facial structures coupled with developments in image-processing will allow us to "age" the face of a missing child, or to portray a picture of a wanted person in different views and expressions.

Finally, while the main aim of this book has been to develop a theoretical account of the processes involved when people recognise faces, some of the findings and theory will undoubtedly prove useful in the development of computer recognition of faces (see Bruce & Burton, in press, for a recent review), aimed at a number of possible security applications. Current systems for the automatic recognition of faces (the WISARD system described in Chapter 5 is one example) are very limited compared with human performance. This may be partly because there has been little by way of "computational theory" (Marr, 1982) to guide the development of representations and algorithms for facial recognition. Further considera-tion of the structural basis of facial variation, and further understanding of how we encode and compare such structures, could provide useful input to the development of future systems.

References

Aleksander, I. (1983). Emergent intelligent properties of progressively structured pattern recognition nets. *Pattern Recognition Letters, 1*, 375–384.

Argyle, M. (1983). *The psychology of interpersonal behaviour* (Fourth Edition). Harmondsworth: Penguin Books.

Argyle, M. & Cook, M. (1976). *Gaze and mutual gaze*. Cambridge: Cambridge University Press.

Baddeley, A. D. (1978). The trouble with levels: A re-examination of Craik and Lockhart's framework for memory research. *Psychological Review, 85*, 139–152.

Baddeley, A. D. & Hitch, G. J. (1974). Working memory. In G. Bower (Ed.), *The psychology of learning and motivation, 8*. New York: Academic Press.

Baddeley, A. D. & Woodhead, M. (1982). Depth of processing, context, and face recognition. *Canadian Journal of Psychology, 36*, 148–164.

Baddeley, A. D. & Woodhead, M. (1983). Improving face recognition ability. In S. Lloyd-Bostock & B. Clifford (Eds.), *Evaluating witness evidence*. Chichester: Wiley.

Bartlett, J. C., Hurrey, S., & Thorley, W. (1984). Typicality and familiarity of faces. *Memory and Cognition, 12*, 219–228.

Bassili, J. N. (1978). Facial motion in the perception of faces and in emotional expression. *Journal of Experimental Psychology: Human Perception and Performance, 4*, 373–379.

Bassili, J. N. (1979). Emotion recognition: The role of facial movement and the relative importance of upper and lower areas of the face. *Journal of Personality and Social Psychology, 37*, 2049–2058.

Beales, S. A. & Parkin, A. J. (1984). Context and facial memory: The influence of different processing strategies. *Human Learning, 3*, 257–264.

Benton, A. L. & Gordon, M. C. (1971). Correlates of facial recognition. *Transactions of the American Neurological Association, 96*, 91–96.

Berry, D. S. & McArthur, L. Z. (1986). Perceiving character in faces: The impact of age-related craniofacial changes on social perception. *Psychological Bulletin, 100*, 3–18.

Bower, G. H. & Karlin, M. B. (1974). Depth of processing pictures of faces and recognition memory. *Journal of Experimental Psychology, 103*, 751–757.

Bradshaw, J. L. & Wallace, G. (1971). Models for the processing and identification of faces. *Perception and Psychophysics, 9*, 443–448.

Brennan, S. E. (1985). The caricature generator. *Leonardo, 18*, 170–178.

Bridgman, G. B. (1924). *Bridgman's life drawings*. New York: Dover (1971 edition).

Brown, E., Deffenbacher, K., & Sturgill, W. (1977). Memory for faces and the circumstances of encounter. *Journal of Applied Psychology, 62*, 311–318.

Bruce, V. (1979). Searching for politicians: An information-processing approach to face recognition. *Quarterly Journal of Experimental Psychology, 31*, 373–395.

Bruce, V. (1981). Visual and semantic effects in a serial word classification task. *Current Psychological Research, 1*, 153–162.

Bruce, V. (1982). Changing faces: Visual and nonvisual coding processes in face recognition. *British Journal of Psychology*, *73*, 105–116.

Bruce, V. (1983). Recognising faces. *Philosophical Transactions of the Royal Society of London*, *B302*, 423–436.

Bruce, V. (1986a). Influences of familiarity on the processing of faces. *Perception*, *15*, 387–397.

Bruce, V. (1986b). Recognising familiar faces. In H. D. Ellis, M. A. Jeeves, F. Newcombe, & A. Young (Eds.), *Aspects of face processing*. Dordrecht: Martinus Nijhoff.

Bruce, V. & Burton, M. (in press). Computer recognition of faces. In A. W. Young & H. D. Ellis (Eds.), *Handbook of research on face processing*. Amsterdam: North Holland.

Bruce, V., Ellis, H., Gibling, F., & Young, A. (in press). Parallel processing of the sex and familiarity of faces. *Canadian Journal of Psychology*.

Bruce, V. & Valentine, T. (1985). Identity priming in the recognition of familiar faces. *British Journal of Psychology*, *76*, 373–383.

Bruce, V. & Valentine, T. (1986). Semantic priming of familiar faces. *Quarterly Journal of Experimental Psychology*, *38A*, 125–150.

Bruce, V. & Young, A. (1986). Understanding face recognition. *British Journal of Psychology*, *77*, 305–327.

Bruce, V. & Valentine, T. (in press). When a nod's as good as a wink: The role of dynamic information in face recognition. In M. Gruneberg, P. Morris, & R. Sykes (Eds.), *Practical aspects of memory II*. London: Wiley. Paper presented at the International Conference, Practical Aspects of Memory II, Swansea, Wales, August 1987.

Bruce, V., Valentine, T., & Baddeley, A. (1987). The basis of the $\frac{3}{4}$ view advantage in face recognition. *Applied Cognitive Psychology*, *1*, 109–120.

Bruyer, R. (1986). *The neuropsychology of face perception and facial expression*. Hillsdale, New Jersey, Lawrence Erlbaum Associates Inc.

Bruyer, R., Laterre, C., Seron, X., Feyereisen, P., Strypstein, E., Pierrard, E., & Rectem, D. (1983). A case of prosopagnosia with some preserved covert remembrance of familiar faces. *Brain and Cognition*, *2*, 257–284.

Buckhout, R. (1974). Eyewitness testimony. *Scientific American*, *231* (December), 23–31.

Calis, G. & Mens, L. (1986). Primary stages in single glance face recognition: Expression and identity. In H. D. Ellis, M. A. Jeeves, F. Newcombe, & A. Young (Eds.), *Aspects of face processing*. Dordrecht: Martinus Nijhoff.

Campbell, F. W. C. & Robson, J. (1968). Application of Fourier analysis to the visibility of gratings. *Journal of Physiology*, *197*, 551–566.

Campbell, R. (in press). Lipreading. In A. W. Young & H. D. Ellis (Eds.), *Handbook of research on face processing*. Amsterdam: North Holland Publishing Co.

Campbell, R., Landis, T., & Regard, M. (1986). Face recognition and lipreading: A neurological dissociation. *Brain*, *109*, 509–521.

Chance, J., Goldstein, A. G., & McBride, L. (1975). Differential experience and recognition memory for faces. *Journal of Social Psychology*, *97*, 243–253.

Clarke, R. & Morton, J. (1983). Cross-modality facilitation in tachistoscopic word recognition. *Quarterly Journal of Experimental Psychology*, *35A*, 79–96.

Clifford, B. R. & Bull, R. (1978). *The psychology of person identification*. London: Routledge & Kegan Paul.

Cohen, M. E. & Carr, W. J. (1975). Facial recognition and the von Restoff effect. *Bulletin of the Psychonomic Society*, *6*, 383–384.

Collins, A. M. & Loftus, E. F. (1975). A spreading activation theory of semantic processing. *Psychological Review*, *82*, 407–428.

Craik, F. I. M. (1983). On the transfer of information from temporary to permanent memory. *Philosophical Transactions of the Royal Society of London*, *B302*, 341–359.

Craik, F. I. M. & Lockhart, R. S. (1972). Levels of processing: A framework for memory research. *Journal of Verbal Learning and Verbal Behaviour*, *11*, 671–684.

Craw, I. G., Ellis, H., & Lishman, J. R. (1987). Automatic extraction of face features. *Pattern Recognition Letters*, *5*, 183–187.

Cutting, J. E. & Kozlowski, L. T. (1977). Recognising friends by their walk: Gait perception without familiarity cues. *Bulletin of the Psychonomic Society*, *9*, 353–356.

Dannenbring, G. L. & Briand, K. (1982). Semantic priming and the word repetition effect in a lexical decision task. *Canadian Journal of Psychology*, *36*, 435–444.

Darwin, C. (1872). *The expression of the emotions in man and animals*. London: John Murray.

Davies, G. (1986). Context effects in episodic memory: A review. *Cahiers de Psychologie Cognitive*, *6*, 157–174.

Davies, G. M., Ellis, H. D., & Shepherd, J. W. (1978a). Face identification: The influence of delay upon accuracy of a photofit construction. *Journal of Police Science and Administration*, *6*, 35–42.

Davies, G. M., Ellis, H. D., & Shepherd, J. W. (1978b). Face recognition accuracy as a function of mode of representation. *Journal of Applied Psychology*, *63*, 180–187.

Davies, G. M. & Flin, R. (1984). The man behind the mask—disguise and face recognition. *Human Learning*, *3*, 83–95.

Davies, G. M. & Milne, A. (1982). Recognising faces in and out of context. *Current Psychological Research*, *2*, 235–246.

Davies, G. M. & Milne, A. (1985). Eyewitness composite production as a function of mental or physical reinstatement of context. *Criminal Justice and Behaviour*, *12*, 209–220.

Davies, G. M., Shepherd, J. W., & Ellis, H. D. (1979). Similarity effects in face recognition. *American Journal of Psychology*, *92*, 507–523.

Daw, P. S. & Parkin, A. J. (1981). Observations on the efficiency of two different processing strategies for remembering faces. *Canadian Journal of Psychology*, *35*, 351–355.

de Groot, A. M. B. (1984). Primed lexical decision: Combined effects of the proportion of related prime-target pairs and the stimulus-onset asynchrony of prime and target. *Quarterly Journal of Experimental Psychology*, *36A*, 253–280.

Dent, H. R. (1977). Stress as a factor influencing person recognition in identity parades. *Bulletin of the British Psychological Society*, *30*, 339–340.

Devlin, Lord Patrick. (1976). *Report to the Secretary of State for the Home Department of the Departmental Committee on Evidence of Identification in Criminal Cases*. London: Her Majesty's Stationery Office.

Dewdney, A. K. (1986). Computer recreations. *Scientific American*, *255* (October), 20–27.

Diamond, R. & Carey, S. (1986). Why faces are and are not special: An effect of expertise. *Journal of Experimental Psychology: General*, *115*, 107–117.

Dion, K. (1972). Physical attractiveness and evaluations of children's transgressions. *Journal of Personality and Social Psychology*, *24*, 207–213.

Dion, K., Berscheid, E., & Walster, E. (1972). What is beautiful is good. *Journal of Personality and Social Psychology*, *24*, 285–290.

Egan, D., Pittner, M., & Goldstein, A. G. (1977). Eyewitness identification: Photographs vs. live models. *Law and Human Behaviour*, *1*, 199–206.

Eibl-Eibesfeldt, I. (1972). Similarities and differences between cultures in expressive movements. In R. Hinde (Ed.), *Nonverbal communication*. Cambridge: Cambridge University Press.

Ekman, P. (1979). About brows: Emotional and conversation signals. In M. von Cranach, K. Foppa, W. Lepenies, & D. Ploog (Eds.), *Human ethology*. Cambridge: Cambridge University Press.

Ekman, P. & Friesen, W. V. (1971). Constants across cultures in the face and emotion. *Journal of Personality and Social Psychology*, *17*, 124–129.

Ekman, P. & Friesen, W. V. (1978). *Facial Action Coding System (FACS): A technique for the measurement of facial action*. Palo Alto, California: Consulting Psychologists Press.

Ekman, P. & Friesen, W. V. (1982). Measuring facial movement with the Facial Action Coding System. In P. Ekman (Ed.), *Emotion in the human face* (Second Edition). Cambridge: Cambridge University Press.

Ekman, P., Friesen, W. V., & Ancoli, S. (1980). Facial signs of emotional experience. *Journal of Personality and Social Psychology, 39*, 1125–1134.

Ekman, P., Friesen, W. V., & Ellsworth, P. (1982a). What emotion categories or dimensions can observers judge from facial behaviour? In P. Ekman (Ed.), *Emotion in the human face* (Second Edition). Cambridge: Cambridge University Press.

Ekman, P., Friesen, W. V., & Ellsworth, P. (1982b). Does the face provide accurate information? In P. Ekman (Ed.), *Emotion in the human face* (Second Edition). Cambridge: Cambridge University Press.

Ellis, A. W., Young, A. W., Flude, B. M., & Hay, D. C. (1987). Repetition priming of face recognition. *Quarterly Journal of Experimental Psychology, 39A*, 193–210.

Ellis, H. D. (1975). Recognising faces. *British Journal of Psychology, 66*, 409–426.

Ellis, H. D. (1981). Theoretical aspects of face recognition. In G. Davies, H. Ellis, & J. Shepherd (Eds.), *Perceiving and remembering faces*. London: Academic Press.

Ellis, H. D. (1983). The role of the right hemisphere in face perception. In A. Young (Ed.), *Functions of the right cerebral hemisphere*. London: Academic Press.

Ellis, H. D. (1986a). Processes underlying face recognition. In R. Bruyer (Ed.), *The neuropsychology of face perception and facial expression*. Hillsdale, New Jersey: Lawrence Erlbaum Associates Inc.

Ellis, H. D. (1986b). Disorders of face recognition. In K. Poeck, H. J. Freund, & H. Ganshirt (Eds.), *Neurology*. Berlin: Springer-Verlag.

Ellis, H. D., Davies, G. M., & Shepherd, J. W. (1977). Experimental studies of face identification. *National Journal of Criminal Defense, 3*, 219–234.

Ellis, H. D., Davies, G. M., & Shepherd, J. W. (1978). A critical examination of the Photofit system for recalling faces. *Ergonomics, 21*, 297–307.

Ellis, H. D., Shepherd, J. W., & Davies, G. M. (1975). An investigation of the use of the Photofit technique for recalling faces. *British Journal of Psychology, 66*, 29–37.

Ellis, H. D., Shepherd, J. W., & Davies, G. M. (1979). Identification of familiar and unfamiliar faces from internal and external features: Some implications for theories of face recognition. *Perception, 8*, 431–439.

Endo, M., Takahashi, K., & Maruyama, K. (1984). Effects of observer's attitude on the familiarity of faces: Using the difference in cue value between central and peripheral facial elements as an index of familiarity. *Tohoku Psychologica Folia, 43*, 23–34.

Enlow, D. H. (1982). *Handbook of facial growth*. Philadelphia: W. B. Saunders.

Erber, N. P. (1974). Effects of angle, distance, and illumination on visual reception of speech by profoundly deaf children. *Journal of Speech and Hearing Research, 17*, 99–112.

Etcoff, N. L. (1985). The neuropsychology of emotional expression. In G. Goldstein & R. E. Tarter (Eds.), *Advances in clinial neuropsychology, Vol. 3*, New York: Plenum.

Fagan, J. (1979). The origins of facial pattern recognition. In M. H. Bornstein & W. Keesen (Eds.), *Psychological development from infancy: Image to intention*. Hillsdale, New Jersey: Lawrence Erlbaum Associates Inc.

Fagan, J. F. & Singer, L. T. (1979). The role of simple feature differences in infants' recognition of faces. *Infant Behaviour and Development, 2*, 39–45.

Feldman, J. A. (1985). Four frames suffice: A provisional model of vision and space. *The Behavioural and Brain Sciences, 8*, 265–289.

Fiorentini, A., Maffei, L., & Sandini, G. (1983). The role of higher spatial frequencies in face perception. *Perception, 12*, 195–201.

Fodor, J. A. & Pylyshyn, Z. W. (1981). How direct is visual perception? Some reflections on Gibson's "Ecological Approach." *Cognition*, *9*, 139–196.

Forster, K. I. (1981). Priming and the effects of sentence and lexical contexts on naming time: Evidence for autonomous lexical processing. *Quarterly Journal of Experimental Psychology*, *33A*, 465–495.

Forster, K. I. & Davis, C. (1984). Repetition priming and frequency attenuation in lexical access. *Journal of Experimental Psychology: Learning, Memory and Cognition*, *10*, 680–698.

Fraser, I. & Parker, D. (1986). Reaction time measures of feature saliency in a perceptual integration task. In H. D. Ellis, M. A. Jeeves, F. Newcombe, & A. Young (Eds.), *Aspects of face processing*. Dordrecht: Martinus Nijhoff.

Frijda, N. H. (1969). Recognition of emotion. In L. Berkowitz (Ed.), *Advances in experimental social psychology, Vol. 4*. New York: Academic Press.

Frisby, J. P. (1979). *Seeing: Mind, brain, and illusion*. Oxford: Oxford University Press.

Galper, R. E. & Hochberg, J. (1971). Recognition memory for photographs of faces. *American Journal of Psychology*, *84*, 351–354.

Garner, W. R. (1978). Aspects of a stimulus: Features, dimensions, and configurations. In E. Rosch & B. B. Lloyd (Eds.), *Cognition and categorisation*. Hillsdale, New Jersey: Lawrence Erlbaum Associates Inc.

Ginsburg, A. P. (1978). *Visual information processing based on spatial filters constrained by biological data*. PhD. thesis, University of Cambridge. (Published as AFAMRL Technical Report TR–78–129.)

Godden, D. R. & Baddeley, A. D. (1975). Context dependency in two natural environments: On land and underwater. *British Journal of Psychology*, *66*, 325–331.

Godden, D. R. & Baddeley, A. D. (1980). When does context influence recognition memory? *British Journal of Psychology*, *91*, 99–104.

Going, M. & Read, J. D. (1974). The effect of uniqueness, sex of subjects, and sex of photograph on facial recognition. *Perceptual and Motor Skills*, *39*, 109–110.

Goldman, M. & Hagen, M. (1978). The forms of caricature: Physiognomy and political bias. *Studies in the Anthropology of Visual Communication*, *5*, 30–36.

Goldstein, A. G. & Chance, J. (1978). Judging face similarity in own and other races. *Journal of Psychology*, *98*, 185–193.

Goldstein, A. G. & Chance, J. (1979). Do "foreign" faces really look alike? *Bulletin of the Psychonomic Society*, *13*, 111–113.

Goldstein, A. G. & Chance, J. (1980). Memory for faces and schema theory. *Journal of Psychology*, *105*, 47–59.

Goldstein, A. G. & Chance, J. E. (1981). Laboratory studies of face recognition. In G. Davies, H. Ellis, & J. Shepherd (Eds.), *Perceiving and remembering faces*. London: Academic Press.

Goldstein, A. J., Harmon, J. D., & Lesk, A. B. (1971). Identification of human faces. *Proceedings of the IEEE*, *59*, 748–760.

Goldwater, B. C. (1972). Psychological significance of pupillary movements. *Psychological Bulletin*, *77*, 340–355.

Gombrich, E. (1972). The mask and the face: The perception of physiognomic likeness in life and art. In E. H. Gombrich, J. Hochberg, & M. Black (Eds.), *Art, perception, and reality*. Baltimore: Johns Hopkins University Press.

Goren, C. C., Sarty, M., & Wu, R. W. K. (1975). Visual following and pattern discrimination of face-like stimuli by newborn infants. *Pediatrics*, *56*, 544–549.

Graham, N. & Nachmias, J. (1971). Detection of grating patterns containing two spatial frequencies: A comparison of single channel and multiple channel models. *Vision Research*, *11*, 251–259.

Gregory, R. L. (1973). The confounded eye. In R. L. Gregory & E. H. Gombrich (Eds.), *Illusion in nature and art*. London: Duckworth.

Hagen, M. A. & Perkins, D. (1983). A refutation of the hypothesis of superfidelity of caricatures relative to photographs. *Perception, 12*, 55–61.

Haig, N. D. (1984). The effect of feature displacement on face recognition. *Perception, 13*, 505–512.

Haig, N. D. (1986a). Investigating face recognition with an image processing computer. In H. D. Ellis, M. A. Jeeves, F. Newcombe, & A. Young (Eds.), *Aspects of face processing*. Dordrecht: Martinus Nijhoff.

Haig, N. D. (1986b). Exploring recognition with interchanged facial features. *Perception, 15*, 235–247.

Harmon, L. D. (1973). The recognition of faces. *Scientific American, 227* (November), 71–82.

Harmon, L. D. & Julesz, B. (1973). Masking in visual recognition: Effects of two-dimensional filtered noise. *Science, 180*, 1194–1197.

Hay, D. C. & Young, A. W. (1982). The human face. In A. W. Ellis (Ed.), *Normality and pathology in cognitive functions*. London: Academic Press.

Hinton, G. E. & Anderson, J. A. (1981). *Parallel models of associative memory*. Hillsdale, New Jersey: Lawrence Erlbaum Associates Inc.

Hintzman, D. L. (1986). "Schema abstraction" in a multiple-trace memory model. *Psychological Review, 93*, 411–428.

Homa, D., Haver, B., & Schwartz, T. (1976). Perceptibility of schematic face stimuli: Evidence for a perceptual Gestalt. *Memory and Cognition, 4*, 176–185.

Iliffe, A. H. (1960). A study of preferences in feminine beauty. *British Journal of Psychology, 51*, 267–273.

Jacoby, L. L. (1983a). Perceptual enhancement: Persistent effects of an experience. *Journal of Experimental Psychology: Learning, Memory and Cognition, 9*, 21–38.

Jacoby, L. L. (1983b). Remembering the data: Analysing interaction processes in reading. *Journal of Verbal Learning and Verbal Behaviour, 22*, 485–508.

Johansson, G. (1973). Visual perception of biological motion and a model for its analysis. *Perception and Psychophysics, 14*, 201–211.

Jonides, J. & Mack, R. (1984). On the cost and benefit of cost and benefit. *Psychological Bulletin, 96*, 29–44.

Juola, J. F., Fischler, I., Wood, C. T., & Atkinson, R. K. (1971). Recognition time for information stored in long-term memory. *Perception and Psychophysics, 10*, 8–14.

Klatzky, R., Martin, G. L., & Kane, R. A. (1982a). Influence of social-category activation on processing of visual information. *Social Cognition, 1*, 95–109.

Klatzky, R., Martin, G. L., & Kane, R. A. (1982b). Semantic interpretation effects on memory for faces. *Memory and Cognition, 10*, 195–206.

Klee, M., Leseaux, M., Malai, C., & Tiberghien, G. (1982). Nouveaux effets de contexte dans la reconnaissance de visages non familiers. *Revue de Psychologie Appliquee, 32*, 109–119.

Kohonen, T. (1977). *Associative memory—A system–theoretical approach*. Berlin: Springer-Verlag.

Kohonen, T., Oja, E., & Lehtio, P. (1981). Storage and processing of information in distributed associative memory systems. In G. Hinton & J. A. Anderson (Eds.), *Parallel models of associative memory*. Hillsdale, New Jersey: Lawrence Erlbaum Associates Inc.

Kolers, P. (1976). Reading a year later. *Journal of Experimental Psychology: Human Learning and Memory, 2*, 554–565.

Kozlowski, L. T. & Cutting, J. E. (1977). Recognising the sex of a walker from a dynamic point-light display. *Perception and Psychophysics, 21*, 575–580.

Krouse, F. L. (1981). Effects of pose, pose change, and delay on face recognition performance. *Journal of Applied Psychology, 66,* 651–654.

Kurucz, J. & Feldmar, G. (1979). Prosopo-affective agnosia as a symptom of cerebral organic disease. *Journal of the American Geriatrics Society, 27,* 225–230.

Kurucz, J., Feldmar, G., & Werner, W. (1979). Prosopo-affective agnosia associated with chronic organic brain syndrome. *Journal of the American Geriatrics Society, 27,* 91–95.

Laughery, K. R., Alexander, J. F., & Lane, A. B. (1971). Recognition of human faces: Effects of target exposure time, target position, pose position, and type of photograph. *Journal of Applied Psychology, 55,* 477–483.

Laughery, K. R., Duval, G. C., & Fowler, R. H. (1977). An analysis of procedures for generating facial images. *Mug File Project Report Number UHMUG-2.* University of Houston, Texas.

Laughery, K. R., Fessler, P. K., Lenorovitz, D. R., & Yoblick, D. A. (1974). Time delay and similarity effects in facial recognition. *Journal of Applied Psychology, 59,* 490–496.

Laughery, K. R. & Fowler, H. (1976). Factors affecting facial recognition. *Mug File Project Report Number UHMUG-3.* University of Houston, Texas.

Laughery, K. R. & Fowler, R. H. (1980). Sketch artist and Identikit procedures for recalling faces. *Journal of Applied Psychology, 65,* 307–316.

Lerwicki, P. (1986a). Processing information about covariations that cannot be articulated. *Journal of Experimental Psychology: Learning, Memory, and Cognition, 12,* 135–146.

Lewicki, P. (1986b). *Nonconscious social information processing.* New York: Academic Press.

Liggett, J. (1974). *The human face.* London: Constable.

Light, L. & Carter-Sobell, L. (1970). Effects of changed semantic context on recognition memory. *Journal of Verbal Learning and Verbal Behaviour, 9,* 1–11.

Light, L. L., Kayra-Stuart, F., & Hollander, S. (1979). Recognition memory for typical and unusual faces. *Journal of Experimental Psychology: Human Learning and Memory, 5,* 212–228.

Loftus, E. F. (1979). *Eyewitness testimony.* Cambridge, Mass.: Harvard University Press.

Logie, R. H., Baddeley, A. D., & Woodhead, M. M. (1987). Face recognition, pose, and ecological validity. *Applied Cognitive Psychology, 1,* 53–69.

McArthur, L. Z. & Apatow, K. (1983–84). Impression of baby-faced adults. *Social Cognition, 2,* 315–342.

McClelland, J. L. & Rumelhart, D. E. (1981). An interactive activation model of the effect of context in perception, Part I. An account of basic findings. *Psychological Review, 88,* 375–406.

McClelland, J. L. & Rumelhart, D. E. (1985). Distributed memory and the representation of general and specific information. *Journal of Experimental Psychology: General, 114,* 159–188.

McClelland, J. L. & Rumelhart, D. E. (Eds.) (1986). *Parallel distributed processing: Explorations in the microstructure of cognition, Vol. II: Applications.* Cambridge, Mass.: Bradford Books.

McGurk, H. & MacDonald, J. (1976). Hearing lips and seeing voices. *Nature, 264,* 746–748.

Malone, D. R., Morris, H. H., Kay, M. C., & Levin, H. S. (1982). Prosopagnosia: A double dissociation between the recognition of familiar and unfamiliar faces. *Journal of Neurology, Neurosurgery, and Psychiatry, 45,* 820–822.

Malpass, R. (1981). Training in face recognition. In G. Davies, H. Ellis, & J. Shepherd (Eds.), *Perceiving and remembering faces.* London: Academic Press.

Malpass, R. S. & Devine, P. G. (1981). Guided memory in eyewitness identification. *Journal of Applied Psychology, 66,* 343–350.

Mandler, G. (1980). Recognising: The judgement of previous occurrence. *Psychological Review*, *87*, 252–272.

Mark, L. S. & Todd, J. T. (1983). The perception of growth in three dimensions. *Perception and Psychophysics*, *33*, 193–196.

Mark, L. S. & Todd, J. T. (1985). Describing perceptual information about human growth in terms of geometric invariants. *Perception and Psychophysics*, *37*, 249–256.

Marr, D. (1976). Early processing of visual information. *Philosophical Transactions of the Royal Society of London*, *B275*, 483–524.

Marr, D. (1982). *Vision*. San Francisco: Freeman.

Marr, D. & Hildreth, E. (1980). Theory of edge detection. *Proceedings of the Royal Society of London*, *B207*, 187–217.

Marr, D. & Nishihara, H. K. (1978). Representation and recognition of the spatial organisation of three-dimensional shapes. *Proceedings of the Royal Society of London*, *B200*, 269–294.

Marr, D. & Poggio, T. (1976). Co-operative computation of stereo disparity. *Science*, *194*, 283–287.

Marr, D. & Poggio, T. (1979). A computational theory of human stereo vision. *Proceedings of the Royal Society of London*, *B204*, 301–328.

Martin, J. G. (1964). Racial ethnocentrism and judgement of beauty. *Journal of Social Psychology*, *63*, 59–63.

Matthews, M. L. (1978). Discrimination of Identikit constructions of faces: Evidence for a dual processing strategy. *Perception and Psychophysics*, *23*, 153–161.

Memon, A. & Bruce, V. (1983). The effects of encoding strategy and context change on face recognition. *Human Learning*, *2*, 313–326.

Memon, A. & Bruce, V. (1985). Context effects in episodic studies of verbal and facial memory: A review. *Current Psychological Research and Reviews*, *4*, 349–369.

Miller, G. A. & Niceley, P. (1955). An analysis of perceptual confusions among some English consonants. *Journal of the Acoustical Society of America*, *27*, 338–352.

Millward, R. & O'Toole, A. (1986). Recognition memory transfer between spatial-frequency analysed faces. In H. D. Ellis, M. A. Jeeves, F. Newcombe, & A. Young (Eds.), *Aspects of face processing*. Dordrecht: Martinus Nijhoff.

Morley, I. E. & Stephenson, G. M. (1977). *The social psychology of bargaining*. London: George Allen & Unwin.

Morton, J. (1969). Interaction of information in word recognition. *Psychological Review*, *76*, 165–178.

Morton, J. (1979). Facilitation in word recognition: Experiments causing change in the logogen model. In P. A. Kolers, M. Wrolstad, & H. Bouma (Eds.), *Processing of visible language*. New York: Plenum.

Morton, J., Hammersley, R. H., & Bekerian, D. A. (1985). Headed records: A model for memory and its failures. *Cognition*, *20*, 1–25.

Mueller, J. H., Heesacker, M., & Ross, M. J. (1984). Likeability of targets and distractors in facial recognition. *American Journal of Psychology*, *97*, 235–247.

Neely, J. H. (1976). Semantic priming and retrieval from lexical memory: Roles of inhibitionless spreading activation and limited-capacity attention. *Memory and Cognition*, *4*, 648–654.

Nishihara, H. K. (1983). Recognition of shape in visible surfaces. In O. J. Braddick & A. C. Sleigh (Eds.), *Physical and biological processing of images*. Berlin: Springer-Verlag.

Osgood, C. E. (1966). Dimensionality of the semantic space for communication via facial expressions. *Scandinavian Journal of Psychology*, *7*, 1–30.

Palmer, S., Rosch, E., & Chase, P. (1981). Canonical perspective and the perception of objects. In J. Long & A. D. Baddeley (Eds.), *Attention and performance IX*. Hillsdale, New Jersey: Lawrence Erlbaum Associates Inc.

Parke, F. I. (1982). Parameterised models for facial animation. *IEEE: Computer Graphics and Applications*, *2*, 61–68.

Patterson, K. (1978). Person recognition: More than a pretty face. In M. M. Gruneberg, P. E. Morris & R. N. Sykes (Eds.), *Practical aspects of memory*. London: Academic Press.

Patterson, K. & Baddeley, A. D. (1977). When face recognition fails. *Journal of Experimental Psychology: Human Learning and Memory*, *3*, 406–417.

Pearson, D. E. (1986). Transmitting deaf sign language over the telecommunications network. *British Journal of Audiology*, *20*, 299–305.

Pearson, D. E. & Robinson, J. A. (1985). Visual communication at very low data rates. *Proceedings of the IEEE*, *73*, 795–812.

Penry, J. (1971). *Looking at faces and remembering them*. London: Elek Books.

Pentland, A. (1986). Perceptual organisation and the representation of natural form. *Artificial Intelligence*, *28*, 293–331.

Perkins, D. (1975). A definition of caricature, and caricature and recognition. *Studies in the Anthropology of Visual Communication*, *2*, 1–24.

Perkins, D. & Hagen, M. A. (1980). Convention, context, and caricature. In M. A. Hagen & D. N. Perkins (Eds.), *The perception of pictures, Vol. 1*. New York: Academic Press.

Perrett, D. I., Smith, P. A. J., Potter, D. D., Mistlin, A. J., Head, A. S., Milner, A. D., & Jeeves, M. A. (1984). Neurones responsive to faces in the temporal cortex: Studies of functional organisation, sensitivity to identity, and relation to perception. *Human Neurobiology*, *3*, 197–208.

Perrett, D. I., Smith, P. A. J., Potter, D. D., Mistlin, A. J., Head, A. S., Milner, A. D., & Jeeves, M. A. (1985). Visual cells in the temporal cortex sensitive to face view and gaze direction. *Proceedings of the Royal Society of London*, *B223*, 293–317.

Phillips, R. J. (1972). Why are faces hard to recognise in photographic negative? *Perception and Psychophysics*, *12*, 425–426.

Pilowski, I., Thornton, M., & Stokes, B. B. (1986). Towards the quantification of facial expression with the use of a mathematical model of the face. In H. D. Ellis, M. A. Jeeves, F. Newcombe, & A. Young (Eds.), *Aspects of face processing*. Dordrecht: Martinus Nijhoff.

Pittenger, J. B. & Shaw, R. E. (1975). Ageing faces as viscal-elastic events: Implications for a theory of nonrigid shape perception. *Journal of Experimental Psychology: Human Perception and Performance*, *1*, 374–382.

Platt, S. M. & Badler, N. I. (1981). Animating facial expressions. *Computer Graphics*, *15*, 245–252.

Plutchik, R. (1962). *The emotions: Facts, theories, and a new model*. New York: Random House.

Posner, M. I. & Snyder, C. R. R. (1975). Facilitation and inhibition in the processing of signals. In P. M. A. Rabbitt & S. Dornic (Eds.), *Attention and performance V*. New York: Academic Press.

Reisberg, D., McClean, J., & Goldfield, A. (1987). Easy to hear but hard to understand: A lipreading advantage with intact auditory stimuli. In B. Dodd & R. Campbell (Eds.), *Hearing by eye: The cognitive psychology of lipreading*. London: Lawrence Erlbaum Associates Ltd.

Rhodes, G. (1985). Lateralised processes in face recognition. *British Journal of Psychology*, *76*, 249–271.

Rhodes, G., Brennan, S., & Carey, S. (in press). Recognition and ratings of caricatures: Implications for mental representations of faces. *Cognitive Psychology*.

Riley, D. & Costall, A. (1980). Comment on "Recognition of faces in the presence of two-dimensional sinusoidal masks" by Tieger and Ganz. *Perception and Psychophysics*, *27*, 373–374.

R.F.—K

Rumelhart, D. E. & McClelland, J. L. (1985). Levels indeed! A reply to Broadbent. *Journal of Experimental Psychology: General, 114*, 193–197.

Rumelhart, D. E. & McClelland, J. L. (Eds.) (1986). *Parallel distributed processing: Explorations in the microstructure of cognition, Vol. I: Foundations.* Cambridge, Mass.: Bradford Books.

Ryan, J. A. & Schwartz, C. (1956). Speed of perception as a function of mode of presentation. *American Journal of Psychology, 69*, 60–69.

Salzen, E. (1981). Perception of emotion in faces. In G. Davies, H. Ellis, & J. Shepherd (Eds.), *Perceiving and remembering faces.* London: Academic Press.

Scapinello, F. F. & Yarmey, A. D. (1970). The role of familiarity and orientation in immediate and delayed recognition of pictorial stimuli. *Psychonomic Science, 21*, 329–331.

Scarborough, D. L., Cortese, C., & Scarborough, H. S. (1977). Frequency and repetition effects in lexical memory. *Journal of Experimental Psychology: Human Perception and Performance, 3*, 1–17.

Schiff, W., Banka, L., & Galdi, G. de B. (1986). Recognising people seen in events via dynamic "mug shots." *American Journal of Psychology, 99*, 219–231.

Sergent, J. (1983). Role of the input in visual hemispheric asymmetries. *Psychological Bulletin, 93*, 481–512.

Sergent, J. (1984). An investigation into component and configural processes underlying face recognition. *British Journal of Psychology, 75*, 221–242.

Sergent, J. (1986). Microgenesis of face perception. In H. D. Ellis, M. A. Jeeves, F. Newcombe, & A. Young (Eds.), *Aspects of face processing.* Dordrecht: Martinus Nijhoff.

Seymour, P. H. K. (1979). *Human visual cognition.* London: Collier Macmillan.

Shaw, R. E., McIntyre, M., & Mace, W. (1974). The role of symmetry in event perception. In R. B. MacCleod & H. L. Pick (Eds.), *Perception: Essays in honour of James J. Gibson.* Ithaca, New York: Cornell University Press.

Shepard, R. N. (1967). Recognition memory for words, sentences, and pictures. *Journal of Verbal Learning and Verbal Behaviour, 6*, 156–163.

Shepherd, J. W. (1981). Social factors in face recognition. In G. Davies, H. Ellis, & J. Shepherd (Eds.), *Perceiving and remembering faces.* London: Academic Press.

Shepherd, J. W. (1986). An interactive computer system for retrieving faces. In H. D. Ellis, M. A. Jeeves, F. Newcombe, & A. Young (Eds.), *Aspects of face processing.* Dordrecht: Martinus Nijhoff.

Shepherd, J. W., Davies, G. M., & Ellis, H. D. (1981). Studies of cue saliency. In G. Davies, H. Ellis, & J. Shepherd (Eds.), *Perceiving and remembering faces.* London: Academic Press.

Shepherd, J. W. & Ellis, H. D. (1973). The effect of attractiveness on recognition memory for faces. *American Journal of Psychology, 86*, 627–633.

Shepherd, J. W., Ellis, H. D., & Davies, G. M. (1977). Perceiving and remembering faces. *Report to the Home Office POL/73/1675/2411.*

Shepherd, J. W., Ellis, H. D., & Davies, G. M. (1982). *Identification evidence: A psychological evaluation.* Aberdeen: University of Aberdeen Press.

Shuttleworth, E. C. Jr., Syring, V., & Allen, N. (1982). Further observations on the nature of prosopagnosia. *Brain and Cognition, 1*, 307–322.

Smith, S. M. (1979). Remembering in and out of context. *Journal of Experimental Psychology: Human Learning and Memory, 5*, 460–471.

Smith, E. E. & Nielsen, G. D. (1970). Representations and retrieval processes in short-term memory: Recognition and recall of faces. *Journal of Experimental Psychology, 85*, 397–405.

Standing, L., Conezio, J., & Haber, R. N. (1970). Perception and memory for pictures: Single-trial learning of 2560 visual stimuli. *Psychonomic Science*, *19*, 73–74.

Stonham, J. (1986). Practical face recognition and verification with WISARD. In H. D. Ellis, M. A. Jeeves, F. Newcombe, & A. Young (Eds.), *Aspects of face processing*. Dordrecht: Martinus Nijhoff.

Sumby, W. H. & Pollack, I. (1954). Visual contribution to speech intelligibility in noise. *Journal of the Acoustical Society of America*, *26*, 212–215.

Summerfield, A. Q. (1979). Use of visual information for phonetic perception. *Phonetica*, *36*, 314–331.

Taylor, C. & Thompson, G. G. (1955). Age trends in preferences for certain facial proportions. *Child Development*, *26*, 91–102.

Thomson, D. M. (1986). Face recognition: More than a feeling of familiarity. In H. D. Ellis, M. A. Jeeves, F. Newcombe, & A. Young (Eds.), *Aspects of face processing*. Dordrecht: Martinus Nijhoff.

Thomson, D. M., Robertson, S., & Vogt, R. (1982). Person recognition: The effect of context. *Human Learning*, *1*, 137–154.

Tieger, T. & Ganz, L. (1979). Recognition of faces in the presence of two-dimensional sinusoidal masks. *Perception and Psychophysics*, *26*, 163–167.

Tomkins, S. S. & McCarter, R. (1964). What and where are the primary affects? Some evidence for a theory. *Perceptual and Motor Skills*, *18*, 119–158.

Tulving, E. (1972). Episodic and semantic memory. In W. Donaldson (Ed.), *Organisation of memory*. New York: Academic Press.

Tulving, E. & Thomson, D. M. (1971). Retrieval processes in recognition memory: Effects of associative context. *Journal of Experimental Psychology*, *87*, 116–124.

Tversky, B. & Baratz, D. (1985). Memory for faces: Are caricatures better than photographs? *Memory and Cognition*, *13*, 45–49.

Udry, J. R. (1966). A research note on children's concept of beauty. *Merrill-Palmer Quarterly*, *12*, 165–171.

Valentine, T. & Bruce, V. (1986a). The effect of race, inversion, and encoding activity upon face recognition. *Acta Psychologica*, *61*, 259–273.

Valentine, T. & Bruce, V. (1986b). Recognising familiar faces: The role of distinctiveness and familiarity. *Canadian Journal of Psychology*, *40*, 300–305.

Valentine, T. & Bruce, V. (1986c). The effects of distinctiveness in recognising and classifying faces. *Perception*, *15*, 525–536.

Warren, C. & Morton, J. (1982). The effects of priming on picture recognition. *British Journal of Psychology*, *73*, 117–129.

Warrington, E. K. & James, M. (1967). An experimental investigation of facial recognition in patients with unilateral cerebral lesions. *Cortex*, *3*, 317–326.

Watkins, M. J., Ho, E., & Tulving, E. (1976). Context effects in recognition memory for faces. *Journal of Verbal Learning and Verbal Behaviour*, *15*, 505–517.

Watt, R. J. (in press). *Visual processing: Computational, psychophysical, and cognitive research*. London: Lawrence Erlbaum Associates Ltd.

Wells, G. L. & Hryciw, B. (1984). Memory for faces: Encoding and retrieval operations. *Memory and Cognition*, *12*, 338–344.

Wilson, H. R. & Bergen, J. R. (1979). A four-mechanism model for spatial vision. *Vision Research*, *19*, 19–32.

Winograd, E. (1976). Recognition memory for faces following nine different judgements. *Bulletin of the Psychonomic Society*, *8*, 419–421.

Winograd, E. (1978). Encoding operations which facilitate memory for faces across the life span. In M. Gruneberg, P. Morris, & R. Sykes (Eds.), *Practical aspects of memory*. London: Academic Press.

Winograd, E. (1981). Elaboration and distinctiveness in memory for faces. *Journal of Experimental Psychology: Human Learning and Memory*, 7, 181–190.

Winograd, E. & Rivers-Bulkeley, N. T. (1977). Effects of changing context on remembering faces. *Journal of Experimental Psychology: Human Learning and Memory*, 3, 397–405.

Woodworth, R. S. (1938). *Experimental psychology*. New York: Henry Holt.

Yarmey, A. D. (1973). I recognise your face but I can't remember your name: Further evidence on the tip-of-the-tongue phenomenon. *Memory and Cognition*, 1, 287–290.

Yarmey, A. D. (1979). *The psychology of eyewitness testimony*. New York: The Free Press.

Yin, R. K. (1969). Looking at upside-down faces. *Journal of Experimental Psychology*, 81, 141–145.

Young, A. W., Hay, D. C., & Ellis, A. W. (1985). The faces that launched a thousand slips: Everyday difficulties and errors in recognising people. *British Journal of Psychology*, 76, 495–523.

Young, A. W., Hay, D. C., & Ellis, A. W. (1986). Getting semantic information from familiar faces. In H. D. Ellis, M. A. Jeeves, F. Newcombe, & A. Young (Eds.), *Aspects of face processing*. Dordrecht: Martinus Nijhoff.

Young, A. W., Hay, D. C., McWeeny, K. H., Flude, B. M., & Ellis, A. W. (1985). Matching familiar and unfamiliar faces on internal and external features. *Perception*, 14, 737–746.

Young, A. W., McWeeny, K. H., Ellis, A. W., & Hay, D. C. (1986). Naming and categorisation latencies for faces and written names. *Quarterly Journal of Experimental Psychology*, 38A, 297–318.

Young, A. W., McWeeny, K. H., Hay, D. C., & Ellis, A. W. (1986a). Matching familiar and unfamiliar faces on identity and expression. *Psychological Research*, 48, 63–68.

Young, A. W., McWeeny, K. H., Hay, D. C., & Ellis, A. W. (1986b). Access to identity-specific semantic codes from familiar faces. *Quarterly Journal of Experimental Psychology*, 38A, 271–295.

REFERENCE NOTES

1. Baker, K. D., Hogg, D. C., & Lloyd, R. O. (1984). *Interpreting medical images by computer*. Report by Charles Hunnisett Research Group, University of Sussex.

2. Bruce, V. (1985). *Introduction to models of face processing*. Paper presented at the International Conference on "The Meaning of Faces," organised by the Welsh Branch of the British Psychological Society, Cardiff, Wales, June 1985.

3. Hinton, G. E. (1987). *Learning by gradient descent: Does it generalise and is it biologically feasible?* Paper presented at the Experimental Psychology Society's symposium on Parallel Distributed Processing, Oxford, July 1987. (Proceedings to be published by Oxford University Press.)

4. Hunter, B. M. (1979). *A study of caricature and face recognition*. Unpublished final year undergraduate project, University of Nottingham.

5. Memon, A. (1985). *Context effects in face recognition*. Unpublished PhD thesis: University of Nottingham.

6. Mueller, J. H. & Thompson, W. B. (1985). *Face memory as a function of rated honesty*. Paper presented at the International Conference on the "Meaning of Faces", organised by the Welsh Branch of the British Psychological Society. Cardiff, Wales, June 1985.

7. Valentine, T. (1986). *Encoding processes in face recognition*. Unpublished PhD thesis: University of Nottingham.

8. Wagstaff, G. F. (1982). *Context effects in eyewitness reports*. Paper presented at Law and Psychology Conference, Swansea, July 1982.

9. Waters, K. (1987). *A muscle model for animating three-dimensional facial expression*. Paper presented at SIGGRAPH, Anaheim, California.

10. Young, A. & Hay, D. (1986). *Configurational information in face perception*. Paper presented to the Experimental Psychology Society, London meeting, January, 1986.

Author Index

Aberdeen, 120
Aleksander, 103
Alexander, 8
Allen, 32
Ancoli, 27
Anderson, 103
Apatow, 31
Argyle, 23, 29
Atkinson, 66

Baddeley, 8, 12, 13, 62, 64, 65, 68, 79, 89, 90
Badler, 27
Baker, 126
Banka, 130
Baratz, 49, 50
Bartlett, 53
Bassili, 130
Beales, 66
Bekerian, 94
Benton, 131
Bergen, 45
Berry, 30
Berscheid, 30
Bower, 62, 64, 65
Bradshaw, 39, 40
Brennan, 50, 52, 54, 55, 127
Briand, 77, 79
Bridgman, 126
Brown, 6–7
Bruce, 2, 8–12, 33, 47, 48, 50, 53, 56, 60, 65–69, 71, 73, 75–79, 81–83, 85–91, 94, 95, 97, 98, 108, 110, 112, 113, 115, 126, 130, 134
Bruyer, 32
Buckhout, 7
Bull, 5

Burton, 21, 48, 134

Calis, 33
Campbell, 27, 28, 33, 45, 112
Carey, 11, 50, 57
Carr, 53
Carter-Sobell, 62
Chance, 9, 11, 15, 53, 56
Chase, 89
Clarke, 95
Clifford, 5
Cohen, 53
Collins, 71
Conezio, 10
Cook, 29
Cooke, 23
Cortese, 95
Costall, 46
Craik, 63–64
Crow, 48, 129
Cutting, 130

Dannenbring, 77, 97
Darwin, 24
Davies, 5, 8–9, 12–14, 18, 44, 49, 62, 63, 67, 68, 120, 130, 131, 133
Davis, 78, 97
Daw, 65
Deffenbacher, 6
de Groot, 77
Dent, 35
Devine, 63
Devlin, 5–7, 57
Dewdney, 54
Diamond, 11, 57
Dion, 30
Duval, 18

149

Subject Index

153

VISUAL PROCESSING
Computational, Psychophysical And Cognitive Research

Roger Watt
MRC Applied Psychology Unit, Cambridge

In this highly original and interesting monograph, Dr Watt puts forward his ideas on visual processing and representation in the early stages of visual perception, and examines the computational requirements of the system and its psychophysical performance.

Initially he defines the scope of the early levels of vision called Primal Sketch Visual Processing, which is involved in registering as much meaningful information about variations in light intensity as it can. This information is then described in a representation which is available for further analysis and action, and Dr Watt examines the computational theory of how this may be done. He then goes on to explore the implications of the data and models , and addresses the question of just what it means to say that the visual system measures spatial aspects of the retinal image, and the effects of distortions. He believes that the calculation of spatial position and differing spatial scale within a distorted metric is not trivial and requires dynamic processes with memory and control. Finally, Dr Watt argues that the strength of the link between the low-level approaches of psychophysics and computational theory and high-level approaches of cognitive visual function lies in the logic of the arguments that indicate the computational need for control. This Essay will be of great interest to researchers in computer vision, perception, cognitive science and cognitive psychology.

Contents: Introduction. A Model for the Primal Sketch. Measurements. Distortions and Metrics. Calculating Spatial Position. Control of Primal Sketch Processing. Synopsis: Low-Level Vision as an Active Process.

0-86377-081-9 1988 160pp $26.95 £14.95

Please send USA and Canadian orders to: Lawrence Erlbaum Associates Inc.,365 Broadway, Hillsdale, New Jersey 07642 USA. UK and rest of the world please send orders to: Lawrence Erlbaum Associates Ltd., Mail Order Department, 27 Church Road, Hove, East Sussex, England BN3 2FA. Note that whilst prices are correct at time of going to press they are subject to change without notice.

BIAS IN HUMAN REASONING
CAUSES AND CONSEQUENCES

Jonathan St B T Evans
(Polytechnic SW, England)

Bias in Human Reasoning represents the first major attempt by any author to provide an integrated account of the evidence for bias in human reasoning across a wide range of disparate psychological literatures. The discussion involves both deductive and inductive reasoning as well as statistical judgement and inference. In addition, the author proposes a general theoretical approach to the explanation of bias and considers the practical implications for real-world decision making.

The theoretical stance of the book is based on a distinction between preconscious heuristic processes which determine the mental representation of (subjectively) "relevant" features of the problem content, and subsequent analytic reasoning processes which generate inferences and judgements. The author is neutral on the question of the mechanism of analytic reasoning, although some discussion of the major theoretical positions in the literature is included. The major focus, however, is upon the preconscious heuristics which are claimed to be the major cause of bias either by directing attention towards logically irrelevant information or away from relevant problem features.

Phenomena discussed and interpreted within this framework include feature matching biases in propositional reasoning, confirmation bias, biasing and debiasing effects of knowledge on reasoning, and biases in statistical judgement normally attributed to "availability" and "representativeness" heuristics. In addition, an entire chapter is devoted to the topic of self-knowledge in thinking and reasoning. It is contended that biases of unconscious origin defy detection because people lack insight into their own thought processes and are chronically prone to rationalisation and overconfidence.

In the final chapter, the practical consequences of bias for real-life decision making are considered, together with various issues concerning the problem of "debiasing". The major approaches discussed are those involving education and training on the one hand, and the development of intelligent software and interactive decision aids on the other.

Contents: Introduction. Selective Processing. Confirmation Bias. Effects of Content and Context. Self-Knowledge. Implications and Applications.

0-86377-106-8 1989 152pp. $25.95 £14.95

Other Titles in the Series
Essays in Cognitive Psychology
Editors: Alan Baddeley, Max Coltheart, Leslie Henderson and Phil Johnson-Laird.

DEDUCTION

P.N. Johnson-Laird
Princeton University

R.M.J. Byrne
University of Wales

How do people make deductions? The orthodox answer to the question is that deductive reasoning depends on a mental logic containing formal rules of inference. The authors of this book have spent several years investigating the process. They repudiate the orthodox theory. They argue instead that people reason by imagining the relevant state of affairs, i.e. building an internal model of it, formulating a tentative conclusion based on this model, and then searching for alternative models that might refute the conclusion. Formal rules work syntactically; mental rules work semantically. The two theories therefore make different predictions about the difficulty of deductions. The book reports the results of experiments that compared these predictions in the three main domains of deduction: propositional reasoning based on connectives such as "if" and "or"; relational reasoning based on spatial descriptions; and complex reasoning based on quantifiers such as "all" and "none". In each domain, the results corroborated the model theory and ran counter to the use of formal rules.

The authors relate their findings to problems in artificial intelligence, linguistics and anthropology. They describe various computer programs based on the model theory, including one that solves a major problem in the design of electronic circuits. Finally, they show how the theory resolves a long standing controversy about the nature of rationality and whether there are cognitive universals common to all human cultures.

Contents: Logic. Deduction and Cognitive Science. Reasoning with Propositions. Conditionals. Relational Reasoning. One Quantifier at a Time: The Psychology of Syllogisms. Many Quantifiers: Reasoning with Multiple Quantification. Meta-deduction. How to draw Parsimonious Conclusions: An Algorithm Based on Models. Beyond Deduction: Rationality, Non-Monotonicity, and Everyday Reasoning.

0-86377-148-3 (Publication Date: June 1990) 160pp. £19.95 $29.95

Please send USA and Canadian orders to: Lawrence Erlbaum Associates Inc.,365 Broadway, Hillsdale, New Jersey 07642 USA. UK and rest of the world please send orders to: Lawrence Erlbaum Associates Ltd., Mail Order Department, 27 Church Road, Hove, East Sussex, England BN3 2FA. Note that whilst prices are correct at time of going to press they are subject to change without notice.

Other Titles in the Series
Essays in Cognitive Psychology
Editors: Alan Baddeley, Max Coltheart, Leslie Henderson and Phil Johnson-Laird.

PARADOXES OF GAMBLING BEHAVIOUR

Professor Willem A. Wagenaar
Leiden University

Why does a large proportion of the population engage in some form of gambling, despite the knowledge that they are most likely to lose, and that the gambling industry makes huge profits?

Do gamblers simply accept their losses as fate, or do they believe that they will be able to overcome the negative odds in some miraculous way?

This paradox is complicated by the fact that those habitual gamblers who know best that systematic losses cannot be avoided, are the least likely to stop gambling. Detailed analyses of actual gambling behaviour have shown that gamblers are the victims of a variety of cognitive illusions leading them to believe that the general statistical rules determining the probability of loss do not apply to them as individuals. Designers of gambling games cleverly exploit these illusions in order to promote a false perception of the situation.

Much of the earlier interest in gambling behaviour was centred around the traditional theories of human decision making, where decisions are portrayed as choices among bets. This led to a tradition of studying decision making in experiments on betting. Professor Wagenaar argues that betting behaviour should not be used as a typical example of human decision making upon which a general psychological theory could be founded, and that these traditional views can in no way account for the gambling behaviour reported in this book.

Contents: Theoretical Contexts. Blackjack: The game that players refuse to win. Objectives of Blackjack players. Roulette: The game players should not hope to win. Lotteries: Big prizes and small expectations. Chance and Skill. Chance and Luck. Theoretical explanations.

0-86377-080-0 1989 160pp $25.95 £14.95

Please send USA and Canadian orders to: Lawrence Erlbaum Associates Inc.,365 Broadway, Hillsdale, New Jersey 07642 USA. UK and rest of the world please send orders to: Lawrence Erlbaum Associates Ltd., Mail Order Department, 27 Church Road, Hove, East Sussex, England BN3 2FA. Note that whilst prices are correct at time of going to press they are subject to change without notice.